RUSSEL AND MARY WRIGHT:
DRAGON ROCK AT MANITOGA

PRINCETON ARCHITECTURAL PRESS · NEW YORK

RUSSEL AND MARY WRIGHT

JENNIFER GOLUB

DRAGON ROCK AT MANITOGA

Published by
Princeton Architectural Press
202 Warren Street
Hudson, New York 12534
www.papress.com

ISBN 978-1-64896-019-2

Library of Congress Cataloging-
in-Publication Data available
upon request.

CONTENTS

PREFACE

In the 1980s there was a magical shop on Greenwich Avenue in New York called Beige Gallery, whose floor was stacked so precariously with dinnerware, it was almost impossible to navigate without causing harm. The proprietor, Stanley Coren, protectively oversaw his prized cabinet of curiosities: a collection that included works by Eva Zeisel Raymond Loewy and a spectrum of Russel Wright's ceramics in various forms and palettes. Upon frequent visits I slowly built up my first set of dishes, mixing and matching Wright's Cedar Green, Chartreuse, and Cantaloupe American Modern dinnerware. Insatiable, I returned for a set of icy blue plates with a matte glaze offset with shiny gold streaks. It was Wright's Grass pattern, produced by Knowles Esquire, that sparked my appetite for Japan and the 1950s in one breath.

In 2006 I clipped a *New York Times* article about Russel and Mary Wrights' home, Dragon Rock at Manitoga, located in Garrison, New York, featuring an image of fiberglass-encased butterflies. It was like reconnecting with an old friend, if not a first love. My eventual visit to Dragon Rock was an awakening.

In the era of TV dinners and mowed lawns, a culture of the suburban ideal, Russel and Mary Wright were artists. The term "American Modern" is at the heart of their story. Russel Wright rejected the Bauhaus's stark aesthetic, a rigid modernism that did not allow for ambiguity, let alone the natural world. The Wrights' story includes multiple binary factors: the urbanity of New York City and the sublime landscape of the Hudson Valley, commercial mass production and the individual character of the hand, Japanese aesthetics and American ideals, cloistered bisexual attraction and family yearnings. Understanding Dragon Rock and the Woodland Paths at Manitoga traces a journey that was just as much an exploration of space as a way of life. This is the story of the Wrights' creation of a haven where the spirit could flourish.

The Wrights met the summer of 1927 at the Maverick Festival in Woodstock, New York—a celebration of music, performance, and poetry where costume met free play among a spirited, international, creative community. Russel Wright oversaw the set designs, staging multiple weekly productions at an outdoor quarry amphitheater, while Mary apprenticed under the tutelage of artist Alexander Archipenko. There, where they were liberated from confining social and familial expectations, the Wrights' love affair began. They soon wed and partnered in the co-creation of what would become a prolific

Mary and Russel Wright, photo for *The Guide to Easier Living*, 1950.

Honeysuckle on Annie Wright's patio

industrial design enterprise. Their home in Manitoga was conceived to be a place to carry forth the ideals of the Maverick Festival, a counterpoint to the demands of their business and urban life. To find the site in Garrison, they took the train along the Hudson River and randomly hiked until they landed on an abandoned quarry, not unlike the Maverick Festival's outdoor amphitheater.

Dragon Rock was developed in partnership with architect David Leavitt, a site of tactile and individual experimentation: butterflies encased in a translucent bathroom divider, plaster walls pressed with hemlock needles, a birch clad door, the incorporation of massive stones excavated from the quarry, and a soaring cedar tree trunk used as the central vertical support. Throughout the property's seventy-seven acres, Russel choreographed a theatrical sequence of paths and meadows, weaving nature into a cohesive plan. Over the course of his multidecade commitment to Manitoga, he developed innovative, sustainable landscape practices. He bequeathed the grounds to the Nature Conservancy for the enduring education and nourishment of the public.

I am humbled to share the story of Russel and Mary Wright and their home, Dragon Rock at Manitoga. Their story is as multifaceted as their output; their narrative often blurred, a little obscured. I do my best to shed some illumination by examining a few strands. I am indebted to Donald Albrecht and Ann Kerr for their great design erudition and to Carol Levy Franklin's masterful treatise on the inheritance of Manitoga. I am endlessly grateful to Annie Wright and Joe Chapman for sharing precious memories of their lives there. I have no conceit of expertise, but only wish to add some surrounding context and deepened understanding to the existing knowledge.

For the first time, four archives—from the Wright family estate, the Center for Photography at Woodstock, Manitoga / The Russel Wright Design Center, and the Russel Wright Papers at Syracuse University—are sourced here to synthesize an appreciation of Russel and Mary Wright's architectural and environmental achievements. I contend that Dragon Rock at Manitoga warrants recognition among the great modernist homes in the United States and that the grounds hold the key to important sustainable environmental practices. I question how it is possible that this wonder is not widely known. I aspire to answer that call.

MAVERICK FESTIVAL

There is nothing in the world more important than the ability to play. This is our saturnalia, our Mardi Gras. There was a sound of revelry by night.
— Frank Schoonmaker, *The Hue and Cry*, 1924

Each August, under a full moon, thousands of people congregated in Woodstock, New York, to participate in the annual Maverick Festival. From 1916 to 1931 upwards of five thousand people poured into the charming, rural town two hours north of New York City, traveling by train, cars, and wagons. They congregated in fellowship dedicated to the arts, including theater, music, literature, and poetry. It was a celebration of otherness, fluid identity, and the spirit of free play. In the recollections of attendees, there are effusive testimonials describing the festival as "Dionysian," "flamboyant," and "fabulous."

At the turn of the century, Woodstock was host to an important utopian art colony— Byrdcliffe, a multidisciplinary art residency inspired by the English art critic, theorist, and environmentalist John Ruskin and pre-Raphaelite values. The Maverick Colony, founded by Hervey White, was an outgrowth. Upon his departure as a cofounder, Hervey purchased land nearby that included a giant meadow and an abandoned bluestone quarry. In the spirit of kindness, room and board was provided for artists at a minimal fee, including accommodations for bartering food and services in exchange for their lodging, welcoming everyone regardless of financial ability. Any income earned was quickly reinvested to benefit the community. While Byrdcliffe was funded by Ralph Radcliffe Whitehead, the son of wealthy merchants, Maverick needed to be resourceful to support its communal ideals. The annual Maverick Festival was invented by Hervey to help fund its survival. It was the first festival of its kind in the United States.

The Maverick Art Colony invited an international circle. Attendees included Isamu Noguchi and Alexander Archipenko, among others representing an energized European diaspora. The robust theatrical and musical programming yielded ample concerts and as many as four plays each week. Maverick's

Meadow, Maverick Festival,
Woodstock, c.1927

Mary Einstein, Maverick Festival, Woodstock, 1927

Couple (identity unknown), Maverick Festival, Woodstock, 1925

Music Hall hosted luminaries such as Helen Hayes, Edward G. Robinson, Paul Robeson, and Lee Marvin, along with Bob Dylan and John Cage in years to come. Gustav Hellstrom, who went on to win the Nobel Prize for literature, coedited the quarterly publication Plowshare, which published essays and poetry from Russia, France, Germany, and Scandinavia. Visual contributors included Fernand Léger and André Gide. The annual publication *The Hue and Cry* recorded the artistic and literary achievements of the Maverick Colony. From the festival's humble beginnings in 1916 to its conclusion in 1931, one may draw parallels to the height of creative output and sexual freedom of Berlin during the simultaneous Weimar Republic era, and the coinciding Années folles in Paris.

This is where Russel Wright and Mary Einstein met. They fell in love in the summer of 1927. Here is where their story begins.

RUSSEL WRIGHT

Like his father and generations of patriarchs before him, Russel was groomed to become an attorney. Stifled at Princeton University and miserable with the constraints of conformist professional expectations, he took a year off and headed to Manhattan and the Art Students League. There he was recruited to participate in theatrical set design for multiple seasons at the Maverick Colony, and co-ran the theater in the summer of 1928.

> *A third work of genius was a circus of grotesque animals in papier-mâché, conceived and created by Russel Wright before he was twenty-one years old. Great square-headed lions did a dance, trained by Ruth Schrader, who was one of them herself, and whipped at by the Maverick starry beauty, the famous young Billie Lemay. There were elephants and ostriches and giraffes in procession. Circus riders performed on mammoth horses that wheeled with their rollers on iron tracks. [...] As we read of Russel Wright's late successes we wonder if he has equaled his first attempt. From my own point, those carnivals were paying for the twenty houses I had steadily been building to shelter young artists in years to come.*
>
> — Hervey White, unpublished manuscript

Alexander Archipenko (left), Mary Einstein, Willy Pogany, Angelica Archipenko, and Eleanor Wolff, Woodstock, c.1927

Hervey had the idea of making a Greek amphitheater of the quarry, so we all helped clear the space on the hillside and made seats of wooden planks. And there we began to put on extraordinary performances, much more elaborate. We all pitched in and helped, we acted, made the sets, costumes and decor. Some of the artists gave away most of their summers in working for the festival, but it was a wonderful communicable experience. My husband, Harry Gottlieb, had worked with the Provincetown Players as scenic director and stage manager, so he was equipped to stage-manage and direct plays like The Temptation of Saint Anthony *and* Salammbo. *When we did* Salammbo, *I was not only Salammbo herself, but for the great Moloch, to whom children were fed as sacrifice, I made a fifteen-foot statue of papier-mâché on chicken wire, which was quite terrifying. Russel Wright worked with me on these sets.*

—Eugenie Gershoy, 1975

MARY EINSTEIN

Mary Einstein, born from a similarly dispassionate elite upbringing, came to Woodstock as a protégé to the Ukrainian sculptor Alexander Archipenko. The daughter of wealthy parents, with direct lineage to the Daughters of the American Revolution, Mary was being prepared for a flourishing future among New York's high society. In contrast, the Maverick Colony represented an empowering, resilient, self-sufficient way of life. Mary found an affinity with nature—with a particular fondness for swimming—and an affirmation of her free spirit and artistic powers. The social and cultural richness of the community in Woodstock became her adopted family.

The Maverick Festival was designed as a garden, cultural soil to nourish new growth.
— Ridgely Torrence, *The Hue and Cry*

FESTIVAL RITUALS — ETHOS

As we explore Russel and Mary's design partnership, and the development of Dragon Rock and the Woodland Paths at Manitoga, the Maverick Festival's ethos provides a crucial undercurrent of their connection and collaboration. The festival informed their shared values in multiple ways: an ethic of working together as co-creators, experimenting with rapid, generative, and nimble iteration, such as the way their first product—a series of circus animals—were prototyped and developed. The colony inspired a sustained dialogue with nature, swift and playful cocreation, and spirited communal life.

Their shared experience at the Maverick Festival was foundational to the development of Dragon Rock at Manitoga, where Russel and Mary carried forth rituals of picnics, identified spaces for viewing the moon, and created a dedicated clearing to form Mary's Meadow. Dragon Rock is theatrically sited at a distinctively similar abandoned quarry, providing stage-like iconic grandeur, while serving as the core organizational principle from which the Woodland Paths flow with dramatic effect. The Woodstock-based festival sheds light upon Dragon Rock's interior theatricality—much like set design—which changed dramatically in response to the seasons.

It is fascinating that the Woodstock of 1969 was born from the same spiritual grounds established by predecessors decades earlier. It is as if the yearnings to congregate among an expressive, progressive, woke community lay dormant until a greater political and cultural gestalt realigned. The Jean Gaede and Fritzi Striebel Archive housed at the Center for Photography at Woodstock is a treasure trove of documentation that illuminates the creative force from this time. The free, communal, and creative ethos of the Maverick Festival is the blueprint to the lives and creative collaboration of Russel and Mary Wright as they set out as partners and conceived their business, lives, and idyll.

Comedy Troupe, Maverick Festival, Woodstock, c.1925

Margaret Sperry (left), John Pascuitti (center), Elsa Woolsey (right), Maverick Festival, Woodstock, c.1925

Various picnics at the Meadow, Maverick Festival, Woodstock, c.1928

Alexander Archipenko (left), Angelica Archipenko (center with braids), and friends, Maverick Festival, Woodstock, c.1927

Unknown (left), Herminie Kleinert (right), Maverick Festival, Woodstock, c.1925

Maverick Festival, Woodstock, c.1925

Art department for set construction, Maverick Festival, Woodstock, c.1925

Sculpture by Russel Wright, papier-mâché and chicken wire, photographed in the Maverick Music Hall, c.1925

The Temptation of St. Anthony, production at the Quarry Theater, c.1928

Giant ship, production at the Quarry Theater, c.1924

Metropolitan Orchestra, "Return to Woodstock Saturday," c.1925

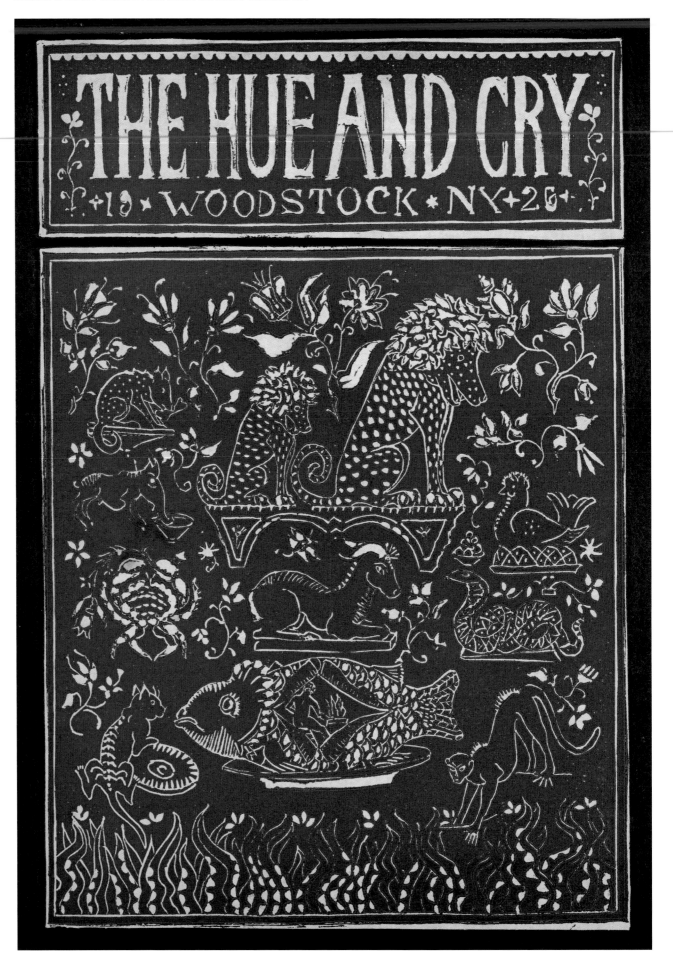

The Hue and Cry, publication of the Maverick Art Colony. Linocut cover by Carl Walters, 1926

Hervey White at the Maverick Music Hall, c.1925

Mary Einstein, Rouben Mamoulian (right), and friends, Sawkill River, Woodstock, c.1927

Mary Einstein and friends on bridge, Sawkill River, Woodstock, c.1927

Crowds, entrance to the Maverick Festival, Woodstock, c.1925

Mary Einstein and Russel Wright, 1927

Russel Wright's telegram to his mother announcing his marriage to Mary Einstein, 1927

DESIGN STUDIO

Soon after their marriage in 1927, Russel and Mary established their entrepreneurial design practice, Russel Wright Incorporated, at 165 East 35th Street and finally at 221 East 48th Street, both former carriage houses). The ground floor served as the studio workshop, and their residence was above. They took the bold, unprecedented steps of branding their work with Russel's name (industrial designers worked anonymously) and established contracts for their works' manufacture and distribution while retaining their intellectual property rights for renewal.

It was Mary's insight to launch their company with the production of small metal circus animals, supplementing their design with a beautifully articulated catalog. Their work and practice grew exponentially and prevailed through the ebb and flow brought by the Great Depression and World War II. Mary bolstered the business with her own finances when needed, along with her significant social capital. The Wrights' vast spectrum of production grew to include spun aluminum tableware; blonde maple furnishings; an array of lamps, glassware, flatware, rugs, and textiles; and several lines of dinnerware, most famously American Modern, for which they are most widely known, spanning two decades. While Russel was the primary artistic author, Mary's creativity was imparted in her own line of work —product development, production, and business growth.

The Wright design studio encouraged extensive experimentation and prototyping, balancing the tactile qualities of the hand with mass production. They took inspiration from the textures and palette of the natural world, including subdued browns, rich forest greens, delicate nasturtiums, and Queen Anne's lace, with distinctive, organic softness to the forms. The variability of the dishes, the way they could be used in different ways and combinations, was radical. Opposed to having a prescriptive singular set, American Modern is playful, iterative, inviting the user to engage with a spirit of agency. One is enlisted as an active, creative participant with use.

In contrast to the chromatic Bauer Pottery and Fiestaware of the same era, the Wrights' ceramics are painterly and nuanced, nodding to the changing seasons and organic qualities with names such as Seafoam, Chutney, and Cedar Green. Nature served as an endless source of nourishment—be it the earth, rocks, blossoms, seeds, blades of grass, ferns, or pine needles— autumnal reds, or speckled grays with heathering and grain derived from granite—all harvested from their Hudson Valley retreat.

Residential divided vegetable bowl, Melmac, c.1953

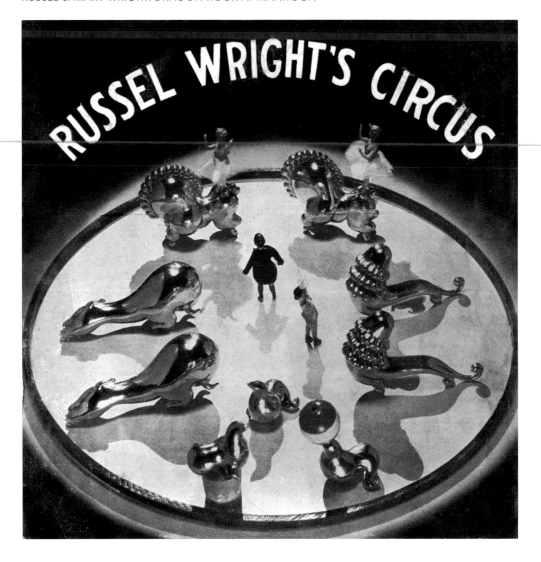

Above: brochure for "Circus Animals," 1928. Below: nickel-plated "Libbilou" horse bookends, c.1928

Mary subscribed to the then-emerging discipline of consumer insight by enlisting testimonials from *McCall's* magazine, which conducted qualitative research. She also oversaw marketing, orchestrating a steady drumbeat of press promoting Russel and their studio via multiple channels. She named the products, drafted the brochures, produced print ads, sat for radio talk shows, made frequent in-store appearances, and packaged presentations for trade shows. Mary leveraged marketing skills inherited from her parents, who were successful textile merchants.

As early as 1930, Mary and Russel established a working relationship with Irving Richards, who managed their sales (he also represented the work of Eva Zeisel). This relationship sustained for decades and was a key factor in their success. They participated in a series of design shows and were recruited to design a food-themed exhibition hall for the 1939 New York World's Fair.

In 1940 Russel launched the American Way, an effort to assemble a coalition of talented design peers and products, building national confidence and pride. Its creation appears to have been motivated in reaction to the ardor for the Bauhaus. Russel found the European ethos mechanical and cold and believed in a North American modernism that embraced democratic values of individuality and self-expression. The program fell to the wayside with the onset of World War II as the nation's attention pivoted to greater concerns. Postwar, the Wrights were poised to serve the enormous population boom with accessible design.

In 1950 the Wrights established themselves as design authorities with *Guide to Easier Living*, published by Simon & Schuster, bringing them even greater visibility. While presented as a treatise on lifestyle, the book is a clear repudiation of the confines of conventional gender roles and class. Their guide suggests a disruption of traditions and instead embraces an ease, grace, ambiance, and quality of life that is accessible and self-made. It opens with data on the hours women versus their male partners spend on housework and encourages equity. (Although Mary nostalgically notes the loss of her cook.) There is a repudiation of excesses at every turn. *Guide to Easier Living* is an argument for the aesthetics of an informal lifestyle, actively bending values and tastes, marking a cultural shift. While commissions, manufacturers, and contracts would come and go, the quality of their works and the ethics that informed them were unwavering.

Above: exterior design studio, New York, c.1930. Below: interior of the design studio, New York, c.1930

Russel Wright: upstairs apartment, c.1935

Serving pieces: spun aluminum, birch and cork pitcher, decanter, and tray, c.1933

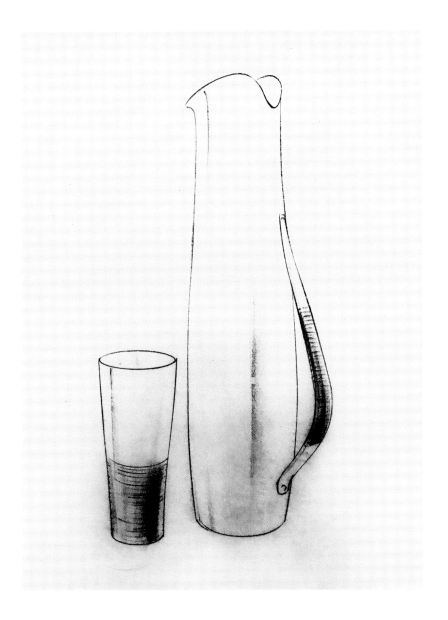

Sketch for Everlast aluminite pitcher and tumbler with rattan handle, c.1930

Serving pieces: Spun aluminum, bamboo, birch, and cork, 1933

Oceana serving dish, maple, 1935

American Modern lounge chair, Conant-Ball Co., maple, 1935

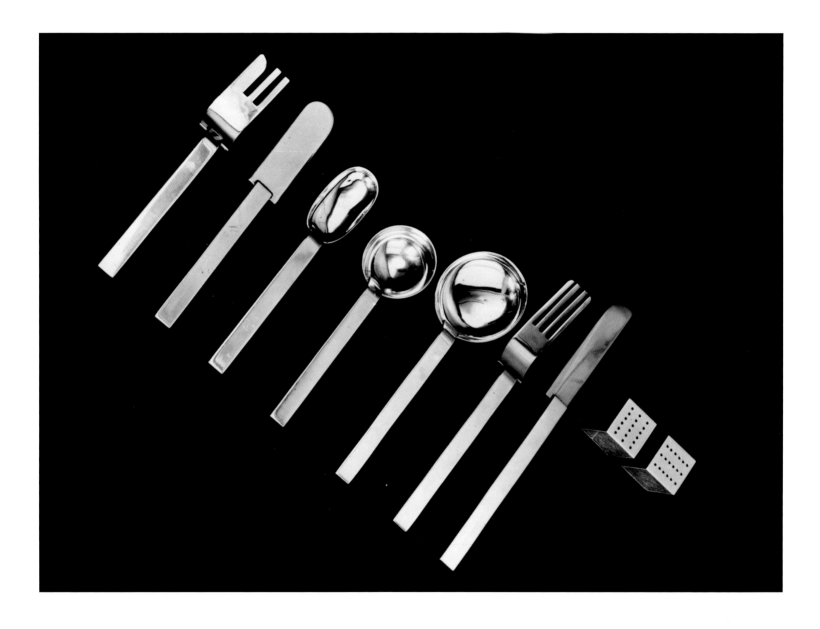

National Silver Sterling Flatware, c.1933

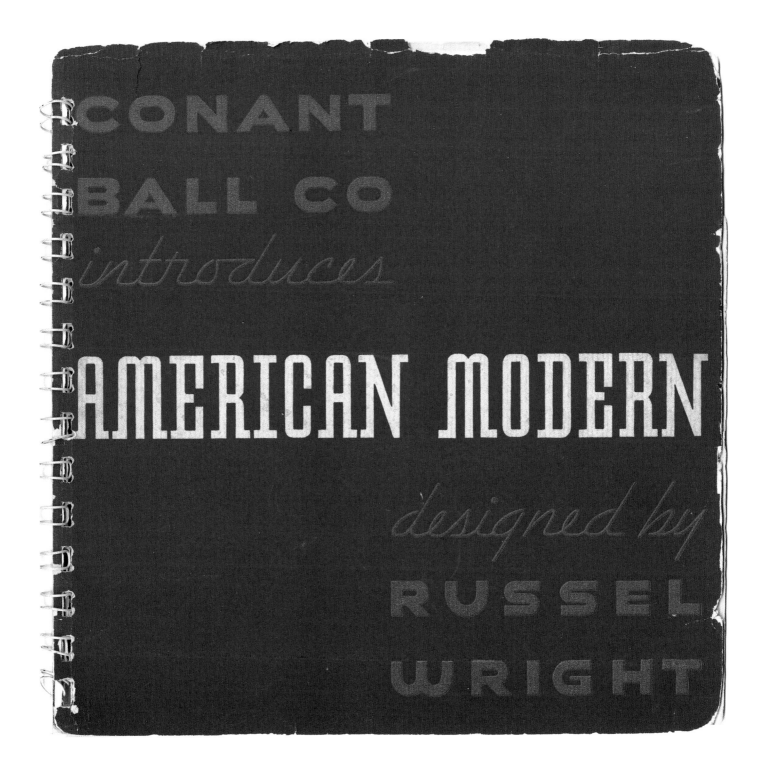

Conant-Ball Co. brochure, c.1935

American Modern dinnerware, Steubenville, 1939

American Modern dinnerware, Steubenville, 1939

Pitchers: American Modern, Steubenville, 1939–1956

Russel Wright, c.1940

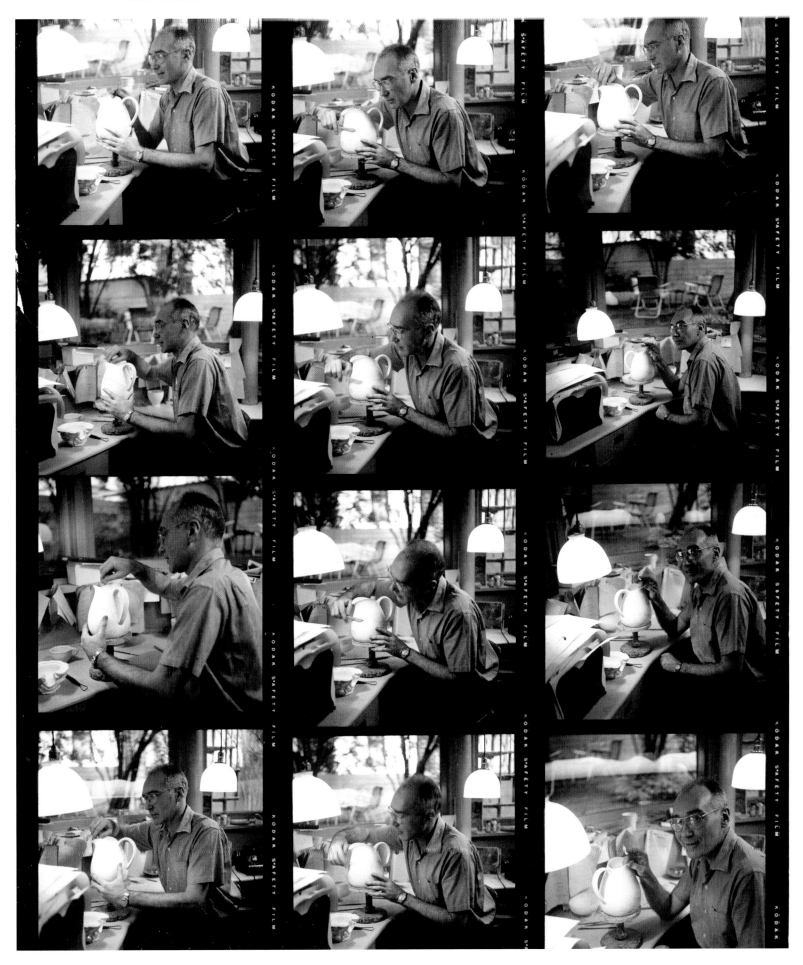

Russel Wright, proof sheet, c.1950

Above: Russel Wright with lobster, New York World's Fair, 1939. Below: the Food Focal Exhibit Hall, New York World's Fair, 1939

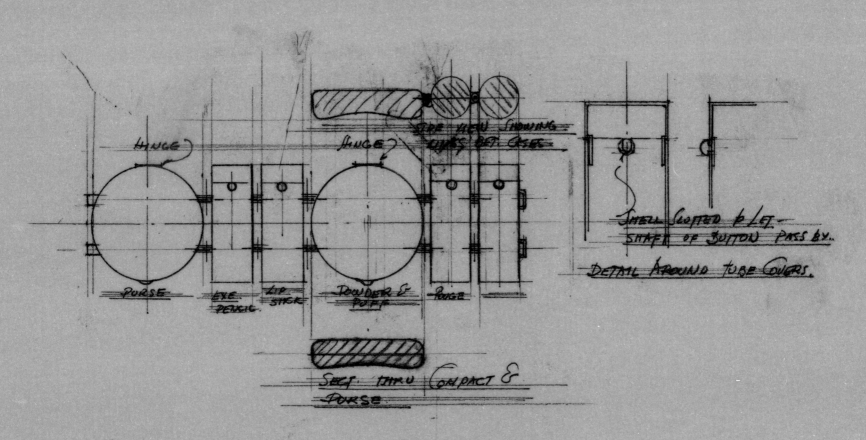

HINGE

HINGE

SIDE VIEW SHOWING LINKS BET. CASES

PURSE

EYE PENCIL

LIP STICK

POWDER & PUFF

ROUGE

SECT. THRU COMPACT & PURSE

SHELL SLOTTED TO LET SHANK OF BUTTON PASS BY.

DETAIL AROUND TUBE COVERS.

LAYOUT FOR BRACELET TO BE USED ON LADY OF THE FUTURE. OUTFIT FOR WORLDS FAIR PROMOTION.

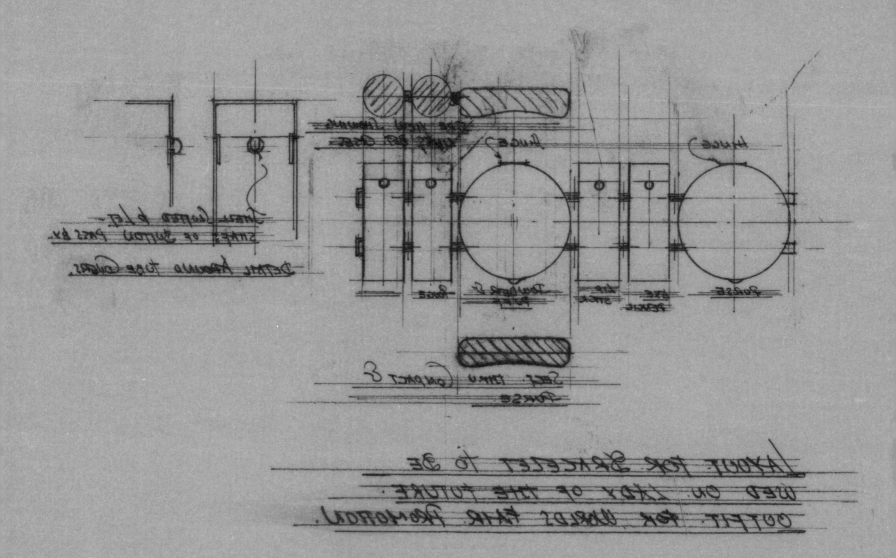

Bracelet, design proposal for the New York World's Fair, 1939

"Frozen vegetables and fruits were used everyday, usually twice a day with fruit juice for breakfast and a vegetable for dinner.

The bride thought them cheaper than canned things and there was no waste.

She never used mixes or processed foods as they were expensive.

Once a month they had dinner guests. About every two weeks they invited friends in for the evening, serving beer and cold cuts.

Beer was the chief alcoholic drink served. Whiskey was so expensive it was served only on special occasions.

The bride used leftovers in salads or stews. Peas went into tuna fish salad. But usually she tried to cook so there would be no leftovers.

Her only seasonings were garlic, paprika, cinnamon, and nutmeg. She liked all sorts of seasonings but said that she had not had time to really stock up on them or use them.

He occasionally liked to cook something like a grilled sandwich. They owned a refrigerator, iron, carpet sweeper, and radio.

The range and a vacuum, which they could use, belonged to the house. She washed at her mother's in a Whirlpool automatic washer but sent white shirts out."

Excerpt from *McCall's* consumer research, c.1940

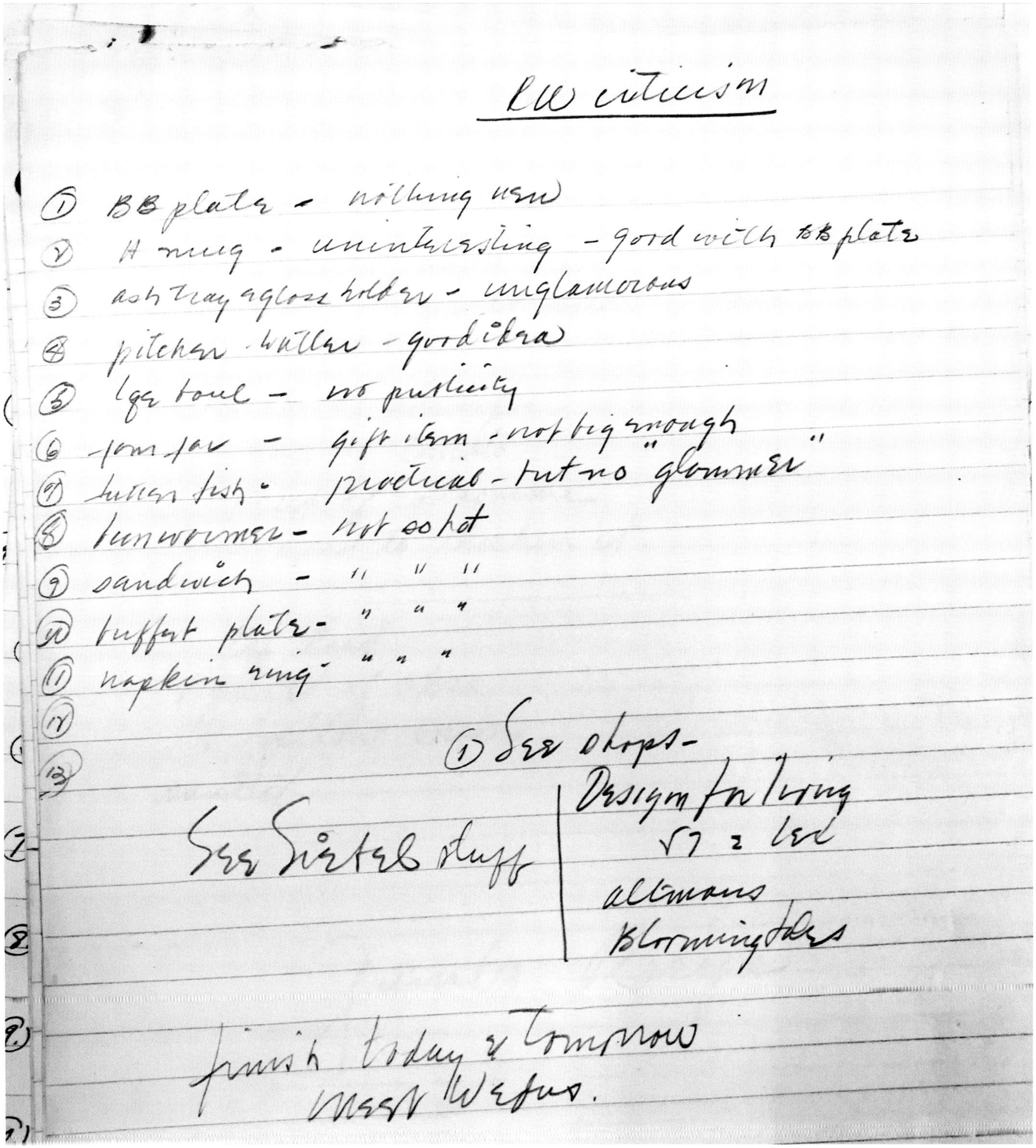

RW criticism

1. BB plate - nothing new
2. H mug - uninteresting - good with BB plate
3. ash tray aglass holder - unglamorous
4. pitcher - butter - good idea
5. lge bowl - no publicity
6. jam jar - gift item - not big enough
7. butter dish - practical - but no "glamour"
8. warmer - not so hot
9. sandwich - " " "
10. buffet plate - " " "
11. napkin ring - " " "
12.
13.

① See shops -

See Sixteb stuff | Design for Living
                  √7 = led
                  altmans
                  Bloomingdales

finish today & tomorrow
meet Wefus.

Mary Wright notes on dinner service, c.1940

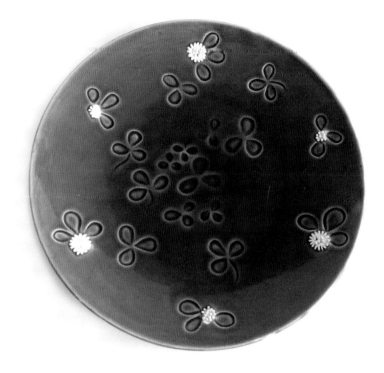

Above: Country Gardens plate, Mary Wright, c.1946. Below: Country Gardens ladle, butter plateau, and wood tray, Mary Wright. c.1946

Mary Wright, c.1935

Bowl, Highlight, Snow Glass, Paden City, c.1949

Photos by Mary Wright, branches with snow, c.1949

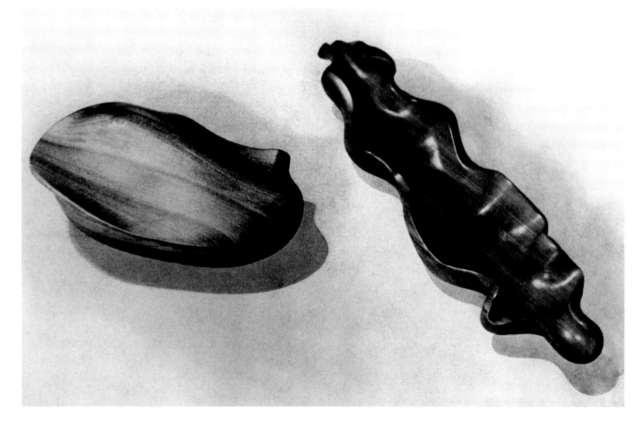

Above: American Modern covered pitcher, carafe and divided relish server, 1939–1951. Below: Oceana covered candy bowl and centerpiece bowl, 1935

Above: American Modern dinnerware, Steubenville, 1939. Below: Bauer vase, ashtray and Manta Ray, 1945

Casual dinnerware, Iroquois China Company, c.1946

Imperial Pinched tumblers, c.1951

Imperial Flair glassware, c.1951

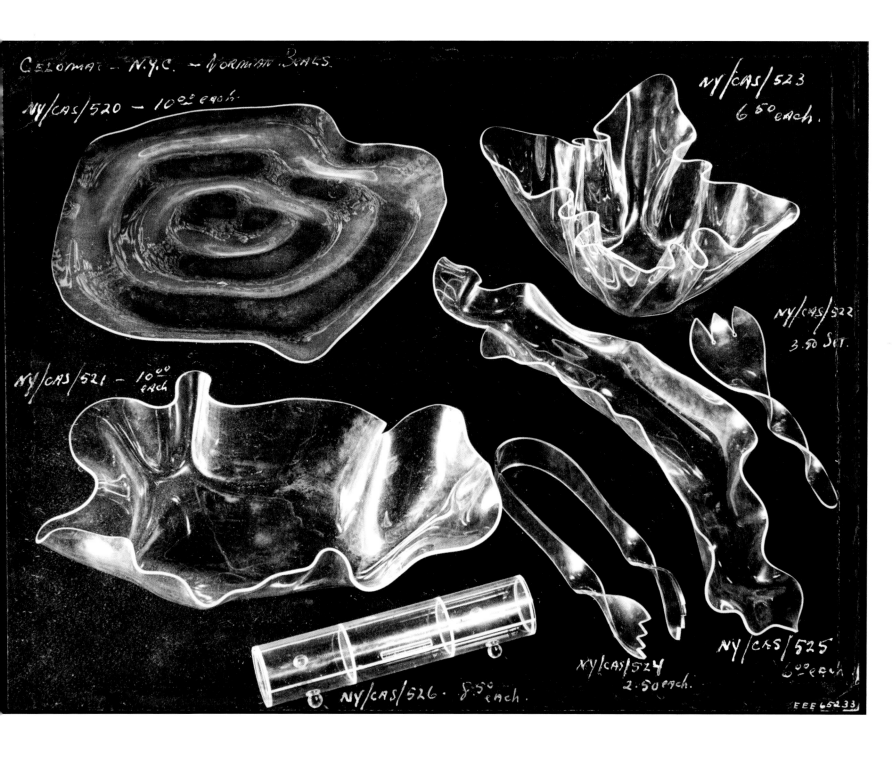

Oceana models considered for use in Lucite, Celomat, c.1954

Nasturtium studies, c.1945

Nasturtium plate and cup, prototype, c.1946

Foliage, study for Knowles Esquire Botanica dishware, c.1955

Knowles Esquire Botanica teapot, c.1955

Foliage, study for Knowles Esquire Botanica dishware, c.1955

Study for Knowles Esquire Queen Anne's Lace, c.1955

Queen Anne's Lace studies for Knowles Esquire, c.1955

Plate study for Knowles Esquire Queen Anne's Lace, tissue with gold details, c.1950

Knowles Esquire Grass dinnerware, 1955

NEWS FROM

Lerrick & Company

INCORPORATED · FIFTEEN COURT, NEW YORK CITY, NEW YORK · MURRAY HILL

ABOUT: **ESQUIRE by**
The Edwin M. Knowles China Co.
Newell, West Virginia

FOR RELEASE ON OR AFTER:

IMMEDIATE

CONTACT: JOAN LERRICK

GRASS... patterned like an oriental scroll

with stylized blades of muted bronze-green and

bright gold on clear cerulean blue. Borrowed

from earth and sky, the cool, serene colors

present a made-to-order theme for glass-walled

rooms and patio dining.

# # # # #

Left: Press Release for Knowles Esquire Grass pattern dinnerware, 1955. Right: Russel Wright Knowles stamp, c.1955

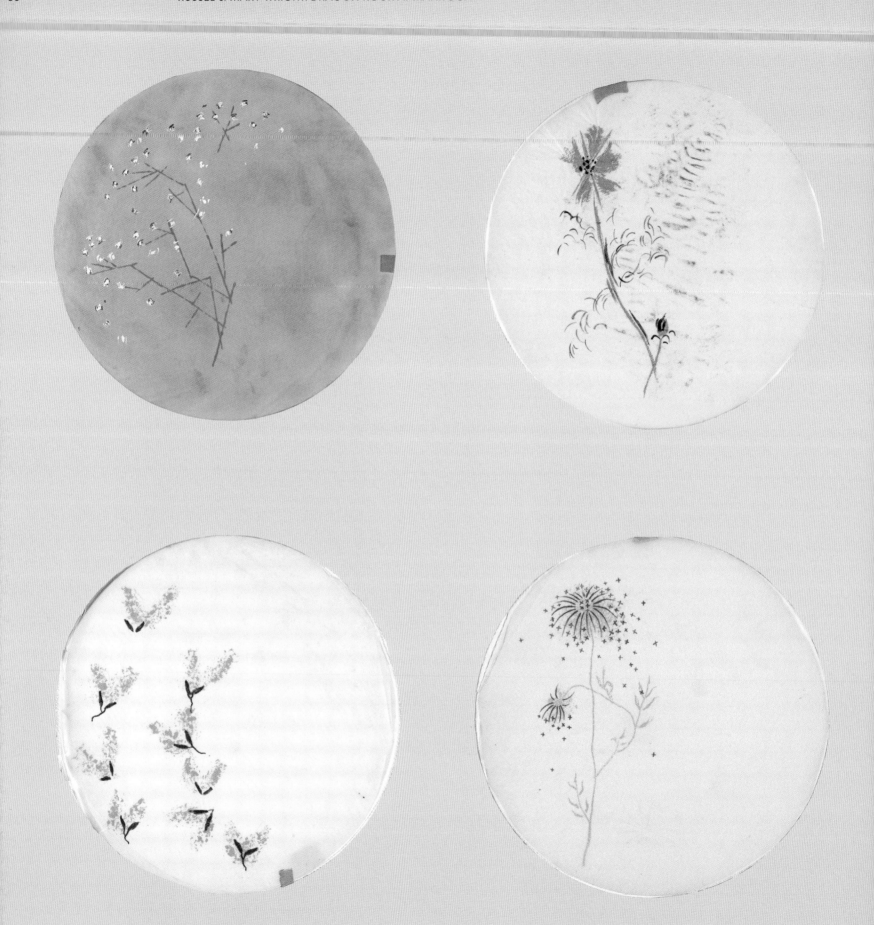

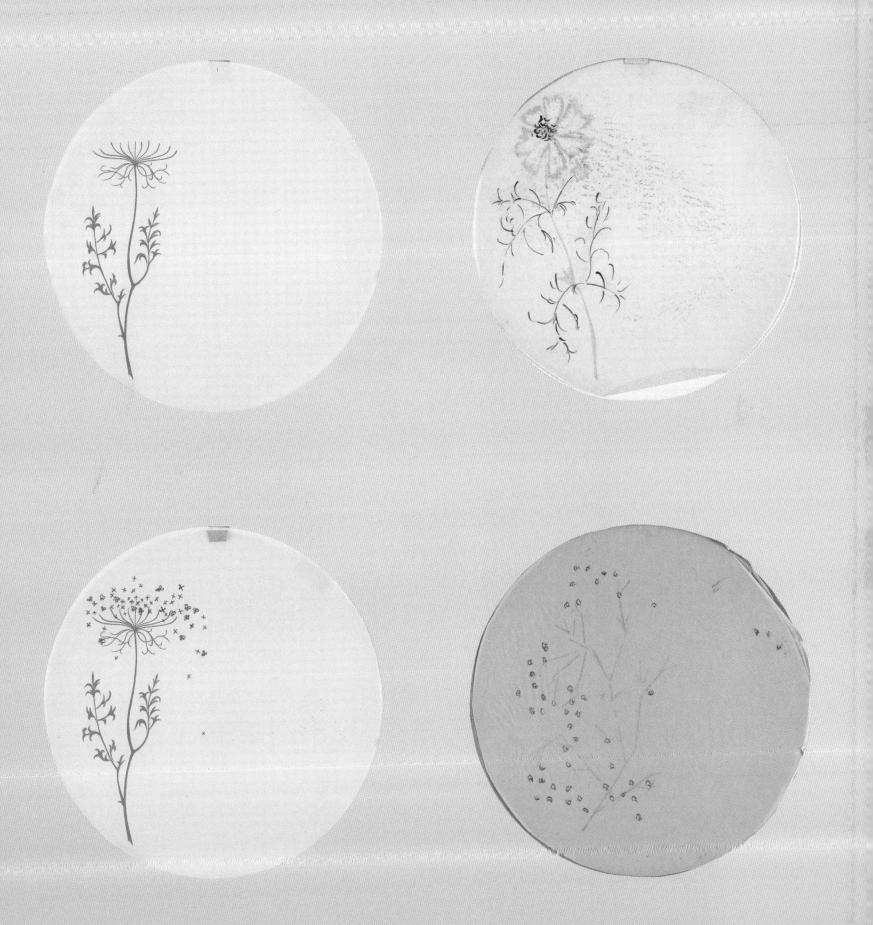

Various designs for Knowles Esquire patterned dinnerware, c.1953

Lamp, possible early prototype, c.1945

Manta Ray, Bauer, c.1945

Theme Formal porcelain and opaline glassware, Yamato, 1965

Theme Informal stoneware, Yamato, 1965

HUDSON VALLEY

The Hudson Valley has a particular North American beauty. The grandeur of the Hudson River, framed by the majestic Palisades, was celebrated by artists of the Hudson River School, who invoked the spirit of Romanticism where humans were diminished in the face of the sublime. Unlike Cape Cod or eastern Long Island—more populous retreats from New York City—the Hudson Valley was relatively unbuilt in the 1940s, when the Wrights first took possession of the seventy seven acres in Garrison that were to become Manitoga. The valley is less about the reflected light found by the ocean, and more about the river, rockiness, and a certain wildness, as the land must have felt even less populous at the time. Although Colonial-era estates and Adirondack camp ruggedness dotted the riverbanks, there were less defined architectural forms in the valley than those found in the Southwest, or even Provincetown or the Hamptons, which had specific vernaculars. Russel and Mary set off on foot into the forests accessible from the train station in search of someplace raw where they could make their distinctive mark.

The Hudson Valley—stretching from Westchester in the south up to Albany—was formed by forceful glacial action. Pervasive storm systems and strong winds battle the northwestern facing property, with snow historically blanketing the terraced topography. Industry ravaged the land during the 1900s, accessing its natural bounty by expanding the paths first laid by Native American tribes who inhabited the region for centuries prior. Loggers plundered the valley's massive trees, hauling them to the river. Years after the forest had been clear-cut, the rich rock deposit then known as King's Quarry was pillaged, resulting in land carved with jagged deep cuts; granite was excavated in a stone harvest and employed for the structure of buildings in New York City, fifty miles south. The quarry's sloped elevations were too great to farm, and the property was abandoned. The land regenerated with wild, dense, growth that enveloped the scarred terrain.

The Wrights' design studio was enjoying its most prolific period when Russel and Mary set out to search for a generous swath of property. Sales of American Modern were on course to be the best-selling dinnerware in history, affording the Wrights the financial windfall to conceive of a weekend home while maintaining necessary proximity to the city. Garrison was on the Hudson Line, only a half-hour train ride to their midtown Manhattan studio, which permitted the Wrights a life that

of the Hudson River, c.1975

Waterfall cascade, c.1975

fully integrated a presence in New York that the business demanded and a retreat where they could replenish and restore. They already had a profound connection to the Hudson Valley, with an annual summer pilgrimage to Woodstock, and maintained close connections with artist Alexander Archipenko and his family.

After years of looking, the Wrights found the abandoned quarry in Garrison which manifested all of the rugged beauty and spatial grandeur of their vision. They took occupancy there in an existing small, red bungalow on the grounds and proceeded to plan their home, lives, and future.

Left: Pink Lady's Slipper. Right: Day Lilies, c.1980

Left: Laurel blossoms. Right: Fiddleheads, c.1980

Glacial Erratic, Hudson Valley, c.1980

Perched atop a quarry bluff, and running along its contour, is an extended linear pavilion. Dragon Rock's glass facade affords a continuous sweeping vista of Manitoga's grounds and waterfall, which pools below. At one end of the building's upper floor is daughter Annie Wright's bedroom adjacent to her caregiver's. At the other end is Russel's study and quarters, a separate structure near the waterfall that is accessed through a pergola draped in vines. The two sides of Dragon Rock's upper floor are joined in the center by a gracious living room, accessed by descending just a few steps. The poured polished resinous floor, or Torginol, leads to contrasting raw granite pavers which continue beyond the glass door facade. This central room is anchored by a generous sofa angled for the view, the hearth, and the record collection. Each room along the Pavillion from Annie's room onwards, opens out to a discreet patio, or moon-watching rock in the case of Russel's studio. This linear sequence at the upper level is pierced by a dramatic cedar trunk, which serves as a vertical rugged stake, with boulders descending, forming cascading steps to the dining area and kitchen located below.

The Wrights' home at Manitoga was conceived by Russel and Mary, but not actualized until after Mary's untimely passing in 1952. Dragon Rock was developed by Russel in partnership with architect David Leavitt; therefore, the lines of authorship often blur. There is a shared affinity for the architecture of Japan and a reverent nod to Frank Lloyd Wright's Fallingwater, and yet the home is unmistakably unique. Russel was well aware of the Case Study Houses program on the West Coast and championed the mastery of Harwell Hamilton Harris's home in Berkeley, California. He eschewed the cool steeliness of the Bauhaus, Mies van der Rohe, and Walter Gropius, and instead sought a warmth that was human, organic, and imbued with the spirit and tactility of individuality. Both Russel and Mary studied architecture, Russel at Columbia and New York University, and Mary at Cornell, however neither were certified. Russel's primary source of inspiration came from his mentorships with production designers Norman Bel Geddes and Ailene Bernstein. (Bel Geddes pursuing the largest projects possible and Bernstein executing the small ones perfectly.) By the time Russel met with Leavitt, the structure's siting and seven-level plan had been determined, where several of the more practical architectural suggestions made by Leavitt were rejected by Wright.

House under construction,
winter c.1958

House under construction, c.1958

Above: Russel Wright, during house construction, c.1958. Below: Russel Wright directing boulder position in quarry pond, c.1958

Being very well organized he had already settled on a site for the house, had dammed up the empty quarry to make a swimming pool, and diverted a stream which ran through the site to create a waterfall on the opposite side of the pool. He also had a detailed survey made with one-foot contours and major tree locations.

His program called for a large two-story central living and dining room, a wing for Annie to the west, and his live-in studio plus guest rooms to the east, separated by a pergola

He vetoed several of my suggestions:

A) To build the house off the ground to keep out moisture—but no, he wanted the house built into the ground.

B) To use sliding anodized aluminum sash on wheels—but no, he wanted oak sash.

C) To handle the drainage, provide gutters with Japanese chain-style downspouts—but no, he wanted the water to drip off the eaves.

D) He wanted a flat roof covered in vines, and I warned him the roots would cause leaks.

— David Leavitt

Every surface at Dragon Rock has been touched with an experimental exploration. Hemlock needles are pressed into the impasto-like living room plaster wall. A guest room door is clad in birch. Each doorknob is unique, whether a stone or wheel recovered from the quarry grounds. Acrylic dividers form partitioned translucent slices that allow for a play of light. Russel formed a panel encasing butterflies for Annie's magical bathroom. He trimmed and pinched cardboard rolls, sandwiching them between pieces of acrylic with a molten texture, casting light in a hallway with a golden hue. Much like the paths throughout Dragon Rock's woodland gardens, its interior surfaces underfoot vary in interest from wood planks to stone slabs. Annie's bathroom is clad in small, square, blue mosaic tiles, reminiscent of Le Corbusier's Villa Savoye. The house's flat roof is shrouded in moss and sedum, a process developed after much trial and error. The cistern, also the cause of much consternation entrapped vermin. Despite such obstacles, the Wrights carved out a domesticated life, one that was enchanted, original, and very much their own.

The choice of the layout speaks to discretion, as Russel was private, both by nature and necessity. Joe Chapman, Russel's longtime companion of twelve years, from 1964 until Russel's passing in 1976, reminded us of how homosexuality was received and legislated at the time. Chapman shared this email after we met:

One question I want to clarify: you asked if Russel and I had an open relationship....we did within our friends, but in those days, just forty years ago, it's hard to believe today, but openly gay life was unthinkable for most people—homosexual relationships were considered a crime and could lead to jail. The psychiatric profession considered homosexuality a mental disorder—The World Health Organization did not remove homosexuality from its list of mental disorders until 1990. The word "gay" used as a synonym for homosexuality did not make it into the New York Times until 1987. The United States Supreme Court decriminalized homosexual relations in 2003. Russel would be amazed, and pleased with how life has changed for gay people.

The theatricality of Dragon Rock's setting is unmistakable. It is literally associated with production design, evident at the Maverick Festival's archive. The Maverick theater for which Russel produced multiple productions was sited at a quarry and referred to as the "Quarry Amphitheater." The essential philosophical underpinnings of Dragon Rock became sparklingly clear, not only bearing the name and physical attributes of the Maverick Theater but also celebrating authenticity, tolerance, and creativity. This is the core, soulful foundation upon which Dragon Rock was conceived. Russel and Mary's connection, shared convictions, and fierce protection of each other's most delicate attributes are crucial to the understanding of this home — the stage upon which an individualist, self-determined family could thrive.

Above: House framing. Below left: Masons on rooftop. Below right: Stone with pulley, 1958

House under construction, winter c.1958

House, entryway, c.1985

View from kitchen towards dining area, c.1985

View from kitchen to the dining area, c.1985

View from kitchen to terrace, c.1985

Dining room

View kitchen/dining area, c.1964

Above: Pergola c.1985. Below: Annie's terrace, c.1985

Fireplace in living room, c.1985

Annie's bathroom, translucent screen with butterflies, c.1985

Butterflies detail

Various translucent screen details

Russel Wright's studio, living area

Russel Wright's studio

Left: Birch bark door, guest room. Right: Quarry remnant as door handle

Russel Wright's bedroom with door leading to terrace

Drawings, house interiors, c.1960

MAY · 61

Dragon Rock, May 1961

Stone "alcove" with ferns, May 1961

Moss and sedum roofs

Living room and terrace

RUSSEL WRIGHT LECTURE

April 1961

As the assembly line encroaches more and more on our working life, crowding out individual creative expression, the need for a home in which we can realize ourselves as individuals becomes increasingly urgent.

Seemingly in direct opposition to this growing need is our great American mass production of construction materials—homes, appliances, and furnishings. We are justly proud of the vast distribution among our... conveniences we produce.

The American home is, I believe, our greatest contribution to the culture of our times. But we have now to solve this great problem of giving our homes and the lives we lead in them the individuality that American democratic beginnings promised.

Perhaps one path to the solution of this problem is in the increasing amount of time which our technology permits Americans to have at home. Our large-scale and growing tradition of "do-it-yourself" is helping us to individualize our homes, and may continue to do so. My own experimental and personal country home is intended as an experiment and demonstration that contemporary design can create from old and new materials a home highly individual, capable of the variety of moods that can be found in traditional homes, a home that can join the emotional, sentimental, and comfort that we have created in the twentieth century.

I have planned and labored hard and long, at so much expense of money and energy, that I certainly am not recommending anything comparable to anyone else. Dragon Rock, the house in Garrison, must not be thought of as a prototype—it is an exaggerated demonstration of how individual a house can be.

I have been pleased to overhear some visitors to the new house say that they wouldn't live in the house even if they were paid to do so. The house was designed for use by me and my family.

I am going to give you some idea of the planning and work that went into the house to supply the needs of the family and to wed it to our particular patch of land. The first consideration in building, I believe, should be the family. Let's take a look at my family. I must first speak of Mary, who died eight years ago, because for many years she looked for the land and helped plan the house with me.

Mary, although a native New Yorker, always wanted to live almost anywhere else. She loved nature, animals, flowers, and music. Then there was Ann, who wasn't around at the time of the original planning; and we had to imagine what a little girl would need to grow up in. But she was around in the final planning; and then there was me. The best way of describing myself is to use the results of authoritative tests. A few years ago, I employed a part-time personnel man to interview people I was employing. He used a fascinating test called the Kuder Preference Test. It was made up of three hundred questions. The applicants were given a stylus and would punch these questions. Then, the personnel man would fold the test and read off the result and grade the applicant in terms of the percentiles of his real interest. I took one of these tests, unknown to the operator, and did it one night in bed, and then put it among his papers. It came back along with the papers of the applicants that he had seen that day; and under the heading of comments I read "Do not employ this man. He is this fit only to be your gardener." This test did truly evaluate my interest; I am more interested in nature

Russel, Annie, and Mary Wright, 1951 (with Morgantown stemware) *than any other subject. Five years after Mary's death, we had the good fortune of finding a nurse and housekeeper, Diana Boyce, from England. Diana's interests have been considered in the final building of the house and she has been a wonderful help, particularly in the planting. She not only loves nature but she has had a lot of experience with planting and has a green thumb. Of course her interests have been reflected in portions of the house.*

Eighteen years ago, Mary and I began making a list of our interests. These are not the actual ones; the original ones were much longer; and they got all worn out as I went through my planning and checked. I noticed that we had some interests in common, like swimming, reading. At the center is a list of special things that each of us wanted. The column at the left is practical features that we wanted. We started this list even before we began hunting for land. Mary wanted swimming most, and I wanted a view of the Hudson—so we hunted up and down both sides of the Hudson. The Hudson River is most dramatic between Bear Mountain and Storm King; the river has several moods; this is a dreamy one—and this is a sharp clear one. I bought on the side of this mountain seventy-seven acres of land, which had been occupied by a quarry started a hundred years ago and operated until fifty years ago. The land contained three old quarry pits and a stream.

I began designing the land almost immediately. It was what is called "second-growth." I began cutting down trees, leaving only the larger ones. Leaving groups of hemlock to contrast with groups of birch or other trees—making paths— learning the shape of the land—gradually cutting vistas and views—until at the top of my land, I got this view. Mary wanted a field; and this picture was taken when the field was almost complete. I cut down hundreds of trees to make this field, leaving only the young dogwood. In cutting vistas like this, I would sometimes take photographs and paint out certain trees before definitely cutting them down. I built a dam across the old quarry pit and changed the course of the small brook to run into the old quarry like this, thus making a waterfall, which I gradually changed into larger steps by rolling the boulders down.

When the water was in, the quarry looked like this. I had cut dozens of big trees out to make the space for water. After this photograph was taken, I did further trimming on the cliffs to reveal more of the handsome granite walls made there by the quarry. The quarry is one hundred fifty feet across in all directions and twenty feet deep in the center and gets more shallow toward the end where the dam is placed. We set up a small shack in the bathing area and another shack on one of the cliffs. It was in this shack that I did most of my drawings for the various designs.

Of course during the summer, once or twice every day, I would have a swim or a float.

In doing the planning, I couldn't make up my mind between three sites so I roughly staked off various rooms on these sites. During the day and or moonlit nights. I would go and sit in these various staked off places and look at the views from them until I finally decided on the site on which we have now built.

These are the files of my sketches done over the period of the original planning time before I reached the final plans. My final plans were given to an architect's office, Leavitt, Henshell & Kawai, and this very complete set of drawings was made which took a little over fifteen hundred hours of drafting time. This was done by my going to the architect's office twice a week and supervising the progress of the drawings. The interior drawings were made by me and my staff. Research and drawings took thirty five hundred of their hours and forty six hundred of my hours. This was the final plan. This was the elevation at the entrance. Actually, the building doesn't show nearly this much because the stonework on either side is set completely into the hillside so that you see very little of the house as you approach it.

My aim was to have this unusual piece of land be the most important part of the whole project. In other words, I didn't want the house to dominate the land. On the other hand, this is the elevation which is set into the cliffs.

During the course of the designing, a great deal of research was done on materials.

In doing the designing, I considered various types of materials. Here are some of the natural materials which are used in the house: lumber, in various conditions, sanded and finished, weathered, rough-cut, or lumber just with the bark removed. Leather, fur, stone, birch-bark, cooper. This collection shows the extremely rich-textured natural materials. I think that they give one an impression that is too rich and too restless. Here are a few of the man-made materials used in the house: fiberglass, formica, foam rubber, metal foil, styrofoam.

These man-made materials are exactly the opposite of the natural ones. The natural materials are amorphic in shape and organic in texture. The machine-made ones have the repetition of their manufacturer; they are sleek, smooth. What I have done is to combine the two. This combination of the natural with the machine-made makes one type of material compliment or enhance the other. I did the interior designing entirely myself at nights, in the old-fashioned way of making a plan and four elevations of each wall, studying out what proportions and what material each wall would be made in and what furniture would be used against it.

One phase, which I can't show in these slides, is the model that we made—a contour of the whole area of the quarry and on it. A model of the house. This model was destroyed before I thought of writing the lecture.

This is only one of the drawings—the one of my studio room. Later, I made color studies of each room in pastel, like this. These color studies were made for winter and summer schemes because I wanted my house to be always interesting; and I wanted it to be cool and refreshing in the summer, and warm and snug in the winter.

The two slides up above show the studio in its summer colors, or the studies made for it. In the summer, I [use] the natural wood floor and natural interior woodwork, and whites in many different textures—the white Formica, white linen, cotton, white sisal, with occasional accents of black.

The draperies, floor covering, and upholstery fabrics, and some of the doors, slides below [sic]—the scheme for this room is done entirely in natural materials: natural animal wools, fur, leather, copper.

Here is the pastel color study for the guest room. Above is the summer scheme and below is the winter scheme.

Here is the study for [the] living room/dining room. The upper scheme is the summer one; it is cool. This is a case of blending, of bringing the greens and blues from the summer landscape into the room. The scheme below is for winter; this is contrasting, using warm, hot colors, to contrast with the cold grays and whites of the winter landscapes.

In many other ways, the house is a study both of blending and of contrasting. In form and in construction it does this.

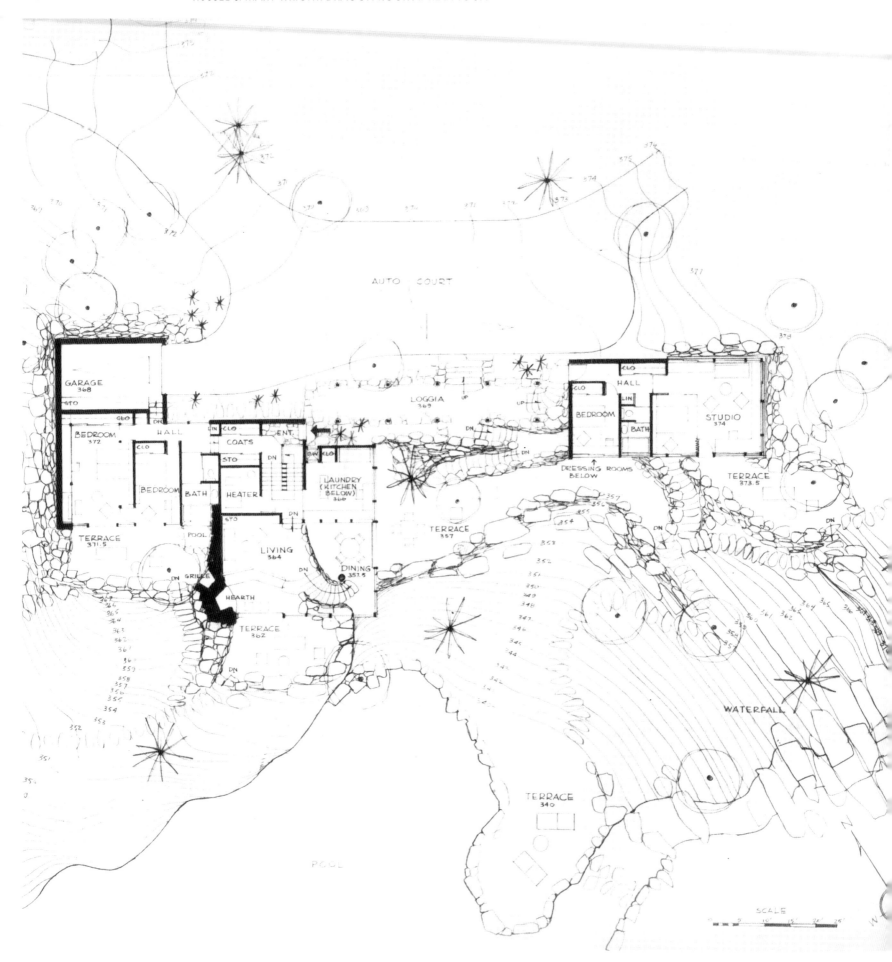

Site plan, Dragon Rock, David Leavitt, c.1957

By blending I mean that rocks, boulders and even trees are brought into the house. The rectangular shapes of the windows contrast with the organic pattern of the landscape on the outside.

The construction has taken about four years; and it has been such a horrible experience that I try not to think about it any more. Working with handicraft labor today in the U.S. is so discouraging that it is hopeless.

The work, of course, began with preparing the site. For three months, I had a bulldozer, a derrick, two laborers, and occasionally a dynamite man. That was in the first year. In the third year I acquired this old telephone truck. With two men, we would lift boulders (often as much as two tons in weight) up out of the quarry to place them around the house for contouring the land.

Only one man of all the laborers who came and went was a joy to work with—old Joe Novara, an Italian mason who worked part-time. He would actually sweep up and was the only one who was really interested in the progress of the house. At the rear of the picture, you see another apparatus used in building the house: a tripod with block and tackle. Finally, the main support of the house: an old cedar tree that I found down by the road which measures thirty inches at the base and eighteen inches at the top. It supports a wonderful beam, which is twenty-eight feet and twelve inches long by twenty-three inches of oak.

All of the framing of the house is done in white oak. The house is built in a nine-foot module. Many of these nine-foot spaces are filled with Thermopane [sic] sliding doors. This is one before the placing of the sliding door; and this is the door that looks out on the waterfall. Scaffoldings were used, and for two winters, I would go up to work with the old mason, using this scaffold or the tripod in hoisting boulders around the foundation and, in this case, to cover up the flue from the two fireplaces and the furnace.

It was during the winter months that steps for the seven different levels were placed. Finally the roof was placed at the end of the foreground occupying the cliff on which the little white shack had stood, and the portico connecting it to the studio in the background. In the spring of 1960, I did the final heavy work on the preparation of the site. Also, the work was done by the bulldozer pushing or chaining boulders to the bulldozer and placing them.

The masonry of the whole house is experimental. I decided that because of the beauty of the natural uncut and aged stone of the cliffs that it would be a mistake to use cut stones set up in traditional patterns of masonry. Therefore, I looked at my mountainside and saw that the mountain was covered with thousands of stones, boulders which had rolled together forming sculptural masses that supported themselves. I have adapted this as the pattern for the masonry around the house. In this photograph, in the back you see the stones as they continue up the mountain naturally. In the front is a typical bit of experimental masonry. I have made a small retaining wall by my studio window by placing some boulders and setting deep joints of concrete between them. The light-color stones are stones [that] have been taken from the excavation. Here is another instance of this casual pattern of masonry forming a part of the actual foundation of the studio. The planting began eighteen years ago, and, of course, it will continue forever because this is the living art; and it is the portion of the whole project that I like the best. I am glad that I began the planting so many years ago. I am glad that

I fought with the bulldozer men to protect some of the things we had planted or that grew naturally around the house because it would seem so barren and it would take so many years to accomplish what I want the planting to do. My research for the planting has gone on during many evenings of several years, studying wildflower books and catalogs. In the center of this montage you see the way I planned the planting. This is a section around the pond in which I have planned the various beds for planting that I do in the fall and spring. Of the greatest help was Diana, who would carefully transplant wild things from the woods and nurse them through the hot summer. Aside from research, my main work has been in digging the beds, with the help of an occasional laborer or weekend guest. Ann has helped with the weeding and the watering, but not without grumbling.

I'll show you a few shots that have caught on. On Ann's terrace, this is the ground ivy. In no place will I ever have to cut grass. This wild vine has grown so thick that you can walk on it. It grows so thick that when it gets too thick all we have to do is tear it apart. The moccasin flowers are doing well on Ann's terrace— and down by the pool—on a very sheer cliff, eighteen years ago, I started these day lilies. There are hundreds and hundreds of them on the Fourth of July. They have grown so thick that they don't even need weeding, and we can let the kids play freely in them.

I left seven sycamores, which make this thick foliage, shading the living room, dining room, and studio in the summer. The big fireplace chimney and all of the roof will eventually be covered with woodbine—a northwest wild vine that is very green and luscious in the summer, turning scarlet in the fall, and is like thatch in the winter.

This is the only shot I have to indicate anything like interior work. The interior woodwork painting and plastering was done by myself with an occasional assistant from the office. Finally, in the fall of 1960 the house looked like this.

Then, came the snows of our 1960–61 winter. Here the pool is covered with snow. At the extreme left, you see Ann's cave, which contains a shower and dressing room and the shallow end or the pool. Then her terrace, the chimney, the living room with the dining room hanging out over the cliff, and the portico going to the studio. From the studio, looking down to the pool and the dining room in a snowstorm. The entrance and the path we had to dig to get in. This shows the wooden construction of the exterior: eight-by-eight white oak with larger members on both sides of the entrance door. The wheel is the old wheel of a dumbwaiter. The door for our dumbwaiter is below the wheel. This is where we put the packages to go down to the kitchen.

At the right of the door is our doorbell, an old ship's bell, looking back from the entrance to the parking area through an old hemlock which the bulldozers succeeded in killing. Just inside the entrance door. Along the portico, I have used huge stones that I found in the old brook bed — and two of these stones were put in the interior at the entrance. The stairwell going down to the kitchen. These baffles are twenty-two feet long of white oak twelve inches by two inches thick. The stair treads are of the same dimension. At the right of this picture, you see our screen of lights of the new panelescent, the phosphorous lighting material [that] gives a moonlight glow upon the entrance. The baffles are set in the actual cliffs; and the big rock at the right here is the actual cliff. On the middle level of the stairway, there are clerestory windows on two sides with this planting box planted with native materials. This picture shows the use of various materials, the combina-

tion of machine-made and the natural. The actual styrofoam installation is shown on the ceiling held up by sanded white oak battens which pass through the weathered oak beam. The wall at the right is an experiment with an epoxy paint in which I have thrown white sand. The window box itself is of a machine-made Belgian ceramic material. At the right, on this mezzanine level, is a tiny room [that] is a lavatory, also a bar [that] has a counter with a double sink for the cutting of flowers. The counter is covered with a plastic laminate [that] I had made from an old Chinese obi [that] contains real gold and silver threads. The floor is of green tile set in black mortar. You draw up the lacquer screen and you see our supply of vases for botanical arrangements and a small shipping department with rolls of tissue and wrapping paper drawers for string and tape. The white door at the left rolls up and reveals glassware for making drinks. The sink counter also contains a small refrigerator.

At the other end of this level is our favorite room: the family room. It is really the balcony that hangs out over the living/dining room. Here it is shown in its winter dress with a thick wool rug from Morocco. The bookcase balcony has a sliding door, which we have made with our own fall leaves [placed] under plastic. In the summer it will turn around and be white with grasses that we have selected from the place. In the other corner is the daybed and sofa. The daybed is for an occasional guest. Under the window is the magazine rack. The curtain across the window is brass wire mesh. In the third corner, these closets contain many useful things. The brass door pushes back to show the washer/dryer. Audubon's Turkey is a sliding panel over a clothes closet for the guests to use. At the left is the door for the dumbwaiter. The copper door contains cleaning materials and the wood door contains the ironing board. The basket is a laundry basket I had made in Taiwan and above it is a spotlight to be used when ironing.

Looking over the balcony toward the waterfall, you see the steps down to the dining room, and out across the living room terrace and out toward the pool to the cliffs beyond. In the main portion or upper two levels of the living room, you see how I have made this room like a cave. The walls and the green are the same color as the hemlocks across the way, two hundred feet. The stone floor, in the lower area around the fireplace continues out on the top of the cliff, which forms the terrace outside. There is a drop of twenty feet from here to the water.

On the lower level of the living room, seats have been built so you can look at the fire, as well as the view across the pool and down to the Hudson. The fireplace is engineered so that I can use fourteen-foot logs upright in it. In this way, the fire can be seen not only all over the room but also from the balcony, and from the outside looking in. When the fire is going full, it looks as though the house were on fire. This fireplace is the burning heart of the house.

Looking from the living room terrace to the pool, twenty feet below—now covered with snow and the kids are clearing it for skating. Looking back from the top of the steps, down across the dining area and into the kitchen. The living room is now in its "winter dress," with the red doors down below the pass-through. In the summer, these are turned around and are white. Above, the bronze panel on the balcony will turn around in the summer to an experimental composition of fiberglass, which suggests a summer cloud. An old patchwork quilt is being put over the cliff in the living room for Christmas decoration. In the kitchen, I have placed the refrigerator centrally because I wanted anyone working in the kitchen at the sink or the

Living room in winter dress, c.1962

counter to always have a view. The window over the sink looks out over the woods and the waterfall. Through the pass-through, you look across the pool to the cliffs on the other side. The ceiling is of styrofoam with lots of fluorescent light behind it. The floor is bleached cork. At the right you can see the counterbalance closet, which contains the main dinnerware and glassware for everyday use. The storage below the counter is carefully arranged for pre-positioning of electrical appliances and the most used cereals, marmalade and bread. Looking back past the cooktop and the oven is a closet with a rack for pots and pans [that] pulls out. At the extreme rear are two floor-to-ceiling sliding doors made of a Belgian ceramic material [that] contain a closet for canned goods and tableware. On two sides or the refrigerator there is a gateleg table that can be used for occasional snacks and is also used to receive the packages from the dumbwaiter that you see in the rear. Countertops are of white Formica.

On the other side of the refrigerator is a small office, desk, lights and cookbooks. Ann sets the table. The round table top is the small one. It can be replaced with a large oval one for larger dinners, or the table can be moved entirely [to leave] the floor free for dancing, because the center post of it merely screws into the rock of the cliff below.

The closet in the cellar and in the kitchen have given me plenty of space for my hobby of setting the table to suit the menu. These are my everyday dishes here. The rust colored casual china, decorated with Garrison's shepherd's purse, is our main winter ware. The blue ware, decorated with the white violets that are all over our land are for summer, and in the rear are some pieces that I had specially made for me in Japan. My "company" dinnerware is this Botanica pattern, and on each piece is a tracing of a leaf of a different kind of wild plant to be found in Garrison. As a matter of fact, both the shape and the pattern were designed at Garrison. The plastic plate is my newest design and contains a lamination of actual leaves. Some of the baskets and woodenware that I use for the table setting [are] my favorite pattern: The wild White Clover.

Night is just as beautiful as day at Garrison. I have done a lot of experimenting with the lighting. I have used fluorescent, incandescent, and a new phosphorous lighting, candlelight, oil flares, and an Indian oil lamp. I have used illuminated ceilings, illuminated walls for side lighting, of which I am very fond, clerestory window lighting, and much of the lighting is on dimmer systems. The lighting throughout the house is thus flexible so that we can have high, bright light for working and imaginative mood light for various occasions. In the living room, it is planned that the light of the setting sun hits the one-hundred-year-old cedar tree....This is a curtain that we made on one Sunday out of two-thousand yards of ribbon stapled to a tape which has been attached to the traverse curtain track. On the upper level, the curtains (which are blue and a grayed lavender color) are pulled. Friends can sit around the fireplace and look out at the sunset across the Hudson and out on the trellis. I am proud of my trellis lighting. I have set into it, up above, small fluorescents so that the lighting is not obvious at all. At night, it looks as though it might be actual moonlight. As the sun sets, we light the candles. This is one of a few chandeliers [that] can be hung on this pulley system. Notice how the long expanse of Thermopane, which would be black and dismal, is masked with the red curtains and the blue and lavender ones.
Out on the living room terrace, we look back at the studio. The kitchen lights are dimmed and the living room lights

turned off when we lower the chandelier for dining. After dinner, if you light all the lights, the living room looks like this [....] Out at the left, you can see the effect of the lighting on the terrace through the purple and blue nets [that] have been drawn. This is the winter scheme of this living room. On the floor is an old Caucasian Kilam [sic]. The red lacquer doors in the summer will turn around and be white. For winter the chairs are fur slip-covered; in the summer, these pull off and reveal the blue embroidered upholstery. The lamp is made of three baskets from three Far Eastern countries. The brass tray is from India.

Looking back from the fireplace toward the balcony is the family room. The pictures are changed with the seasons and various occasions. At the left is an old Chinese scroll showing Buddha meditating in the forest.

Out on Ann's terrace in the winter… Mary wanted a terrace from which she could watch the moon. The masonry at the right, which contains the chimney and an outdoor fireplace, is planned so the moon rises over it and throws its light across the stones onto this small terrace. We call this section of the house "the harem." The entry is from the main entrance of the building. At the right is a twelve foot long and ten-foot-high closet that will take care of coats, books, skates. The wall at the left is an experiment of epoxy with white sand. The green wall is an experiment of epoxy with white sand. The green wall is an experiment done with fluorescent paint under broad bands of scotch tape. The little statuette on the left is an ivory carving from Vietnam of the Goddess of the Fairies. Another or Caesarian entrance to the harem is from the garage. This is one of two stations in the house for the arranging of botanica and objects. It is a two-and-a-half-inch plastic which I designed to suggest leaves. The entrance to the girls' dressing room and bath, like all of the laminations in the house, is made of material supplied from Garrison. Here are viburnum leaves and blossoms from Queen Anne's lace. On the other side of the door, you look into the toilet compartment where we have used maidenhair ferns laminated in the plastic. These two screens fold one over the other making another pattern—and here is the entrance to the bath itself with a collection of butterflies, which I brought back from Taiwan and Brazil.

In the bathroom, for Saturday nights, I gave the girls this bubble bath treat.

Here is the source of the water coming out of the rocks and at the right is the towel rack made of one of our dogwood trees. The hallway in the harem leads at the end to Ann's room. On the right are the summer and winter closets, an experiment with plastic extrusions. At the left is the door to the housekeeper's room, and because she is fond of bird lore, I set into the wall an original Audubon showing a wren nesting in the mountain laurel—a scene that we often see on the property. In her room, I have stapled a lavender colored fabric to the wall and ceiling. The accessories are Oriental and English and American antiques. The curtain at the window is made of two layers of net, one a bright aqua and the other a pink color   the combination created a pearlescent or iridescent effect.

In Ann's room, the walls and ceiling are of a pink metallic paper, which has a magical effect of bringing outside light into this rather dark room and of flattering its occupants. The curtains here are of embroidered Swiss organdy. The rug is a braided one. This room is planned to change with Ann during her girlhood at least three times. The posts are removable to change the arrangement of the room. Here is one of the typical drawer sections that we have used throughout the

Above: Living room terrace with blooming laurels, c.1970. Below: Dragon Rock in snow, c.1965

house. The interiors of the drawers are of rolled plastics. In all of the bedrooms and in some of the other rooms, I have created side lighting from the closets because I wanted to have plenty of light in the closets. I have made use of it in general lighting of the room by using translucent curtain materials over the closets. There is a fourteen-foot long work area and desk for Ann with drawers below and pegboard wall. This she calls her "mess area," and she can leave it in whatever condition she wants because all we have to do is pull down this roller shade [that] was designed by one of my assistants, but he condescended [sic] to me to make all of the birds native Garrison ones. The back of the sofa folds up for use as a double-decker for a visiting friend.

Here is the entrance to my section, the studio building, at night. On the right is another one of the botanical arrangement shelves, and the translucent material in back is one specially made by Dow Chemical [that] changes from winter to summer. The winter side, seen here, has a copper color. At the other end of the building, you can look down into my room which is a conglomeration of a very large L-shaped drafting desk, a rocking chair from my hometown, pieces of sculpture from Cambodia, objects from China. Here is a corner of the room in the day.

This room has two contrasting types of views. As a matter of fact, it is like a summer house in the summer because practically all of the windows open up—some slide one over the other—and three of them drop down into the sill. This side of the room gives a worm's-eye view up into the woods. Here is the guest room by day. By night you pull the roller shade that we have textured in a bronze color. The corner of my room, in the winter scheme, has this Audubon fox of the same type that we see on the property. The bed cover is from Peru. The bed is raised so that I can better see the view outside.

Looking up from the bed, my ceiling shows partial foam rubber continuing up from the wall at the back of the bed and then a part that is thick with long pine needles.

Throughout the house, I have attempted to make the ceilings interesting because ceilings are such large areas that are neglected in our times. At the left of my bed, I can look up into the woods like this on a snowy day.

From the right side, I can look out like this over the pool and down to the Hudson and the hills beyond.

At the entrance to my bathroom, to the right, is the linen closet. The tambour door is covered with an all-silk scroll from Korea. In opening the door, I wish you could smell the aromatic odor of dead cedar. It amuses me when people immediately say, "Oh, you have a Japanese bathroom," because there is nothing Japanese about this. The whole concept was taken from a roomette car.

The six foot window slides down into the sill from this window. I can look down over the Hudson.

Russel was inconsolable with the loss of Mary, who succumbed in 1952 to a yearslong battle with breast cancer. He lost his wife, partner, and confidant in life, the steward of their business and the mother of their child. He was bereaved, having to muster both inner and external resources to survive. Annie, only two upon losing her mother, for a while lived with the family of Rem Wurlitzer—a client and longtime friend. In 1955 Russel took on a consultancy project for the US State Department and left for Southeast Asia for a recuperative getaway. Eventually, Russel and Annie's new family paradigm became normalized, and humor was restored. They found their rhythm together.

Food played a vibrant role in the Wright household. Before the culture of celebrity chefs, such as Julia Child, Jacques Pépin, and Craig Claiborne of the *New York Times*, there were just a few exceptional restaurants in New York, and the art of cooking at home. The Wrights relished both.

While Mary did not seem to have the time or much interest in cooking, Russel loved sumptuous dining, the more theatrical the better: curry with shaved coconut, grapes, and chutneys; salmon soufflé; or roast duck strewn with chrysanthemum petals for dramatic effect.

Mamie Mitchell joined the Wrights as a companion for Annie as a toddler and to help support the household. While an important part of her scope was to prepare meals, her repertoire was limited to meatballs, spaghetti, and chocolate pudding. Russel took ten days off of work to prepare for her a fastidious recipe book, a hand-typed bible of food preparation and menus with coordinated dinnerware, differentiated for the city and Garrison, including table settings, napkins, and linens when hosting company.

At first glance, the cookbook feels very prescriptive, beyond that of a single father seeking to manage a household. But upon examination, it is clear that this book is a work of artistry, the imagination of an alchemist who delighted pairing tastes and cultures with palettes and creating ambiance with dishware, fabrics, lighting, and textures. Russel considered every detail with discerning care to create a harmonizing effect. He honored the bounty of each season, with cool, crisp salads served on white in the summer and warming root vegetables in the winter. The original spiral-bound book with its fastidious notation is a blueprint for daily family ritual, an act of expansive curiosity and love. Before long, Mamie was preparing marvelous stews, packed to travel for the weekend in the country, plated on chutney brown America Modern dishes, and served by candlelight as designed.

Dragon Rock, Life Magazine, c.1962

When Annie was five, Diana Boyce Young picked up where Mitchell left off, fully embracing all of Russel's specificity. Her tour of duty coincided with the development of the house itself and she took great pride in its operations. Labels appeared in the kitchen differentiating the serving implements from the soup spoons, butter knives from dinner knives. Labeled designations were assigned to Russel's dressers, differentiating winter socks from summer socks, winter pajamas from those of the cooler seasons.

But the ritual Diana most eagerly embraced was turning over the house from one season to the other, a significant undertaking that she assumed twice a year. The overall motif was white for summer and warm orange and red tones for winter. Whole cabinet panels would be turned from one side to another. That included the storage panels in the living room and in Russel's studio, the honeycombed fiberglass in the hall, and the largest panel of all, over the kitchen threshold framing the mezzanine. The latter converted from a refreshing white in the summer to a gleaming warm copper when the temperature cooled, requiring a huge ladder to turn it over. As an ardent collaborator, she worked with Russel to change all the textiles with slipcovers, including bedspreads and pillows. Blue Danish woven upholstery on the living room chairs were covered with sheepskins for warmth. There was a summer chandelier—a pair of spacecraft-like, icy blue forms—that was replaced with an iron-cast candelabra in winter. The artwork changed too. An Audubon print of a black crow in the mezzanine was switched out with a wild turkey. An owl in the study was swapped for a fox. And in the winter months, long flowing curtains of red ribbons took the place of a delicate light-toned Jack Lenor Larsen fabric that was woven at the top and bottom with open threads in the center allowing for an expansive view.

The rituals at Manitoga also included a fondness for picnics as weather permitted, Annie Wright recalls:

Russel did really love picnics. All over the place. It really depended on who was around as to how strenuous the hike was. Not everyone wanted to climb the mountain, so to speak. One of his favorite spots to "hike" was across from the house above the quarry pond. It was called "the secret room." You could reach it by stone steps he put in and was cozy with moss blanketing the rocks and walls. I don't remember that the food was

Annie and Russel Wright cooking, c.1962

Summer light fixture and white ribbons

Russel Wright, Annie, and friends, winter candelabra and red ribbons, c.1962

anything unusual. Sandwiches, iced tea, lemonade. Fresh fruit, as well. Anyway, there were tons of hemlock trees there, so that if you sat in between the trees, you could see out, but no one could see in. He really loved that, and so did I.

Music filled the house and the quarry pond, as speakers were installed by the waterfall. The Wrights had an ample classical collection, as Mary was president of the Bach Society. Musical tastes included a favorite calypso LP and a passion for soloists including Harry Belafonte, Yma Sumac, Libby Holman, and Marian Anderson.

It was natural that the Wrights, arguably the nation's foremost dinnerware experts, had a deep appreciation of food, and a web of culinary talent were integral to the Wrights' social sphere. Margaret Spader, a nutritionist and home economist, became a lifelong friend to the family. Tom Margittai, once a tenant of the Wrights and a dishwasher at the Waldorf Astoria, climbed the ranks to co-owner of the famed Four Seasons Restaurant in the Seagram Building. Russel befriended Florence Lin, who taught Chinese cooking at New York's China Institute, and became very good friends with George Lang, the founder of Café des Artistes on the Upper West Side, where father and daughter enjoyed regular Sunday night dinners.

As Annie grew, Russel's commute to New York City lost its luster, and his business gradually tapered. Beleaguered by continual public-relations appearances to espouse the virtues of Melmac dinnerware at garden parties, his papers at Syracuse seethe with fatigue over being continually conscripted to oblige mandates not his own. Russel ultimately closed the office in 1967 and relocated to Manitoga full time. The New York City chapter concluded, and it was time to begin anew.

Margaret Spader and Turk at Dragon Rock across from the quarry, c.1965

Russel, Annie Wright, and friend with Turk, c.1962

Russel Wright and Margaret Spader, seasonal turnover, c.1965

Russel Wright reversing and sweeping the copper panel, c.1965

Russel Wright, Japan, c.1953

Joe Chapman with picnic at waterfall, c.1970

INTER-OFFICE MEMORANDUM

DATE:

FROM:

TO:

SUBJECT:

Here's an example of one of the most used of my menus. Notice
the recepies and the portions that specifies the table setting,
both for my New York home and my country home.

Weekend breakfasts are somewhat a different proposition. In
general they don't need to be so hurried, but generally there is
somebody who is a late riser, or there may be guests that you
feel that you have to wait for. In our

of begining a day, more pleasantly and efficiently, here are
my suggestions. At the time ʄ of setting the table for the
majority, set a place in the kitchen for the late riser; leave
out the ingredients for him to make up his breakfast and to
proceed with having your breakfast with whatever cleanup you do
and on to your morning tasks; or if there are a number of late
risers or guests, you can leave a 'make-it-yourself' setup in
the kitchen or a dining room buffet or counter. Here's one left
for my guests on my dining room counter andxthe in my country
house, Dragon Rock. Slide # _____.

Also at Dragon Rock, I have a small two foot by two foot compartment
                                    hidden
of a chest which is a/kitchenetteb for the making of breakfasts
for two. This is near my guest room, in a separate part of the
house. In his way, any two guests of mine can rise when they
feel like and make their own breakfast without inconvenience to
anybody in the kitchen.

In the country, with or without guests I employ the simply simple
variations which add pleasure to breakfast, and in addition we will
occasion on a cold or disagreeable morning put everything on trays
and have breakfast around the fireplace, Slide # _____.

Russel Wright's breakfast memo, c.1965

Annie Wright lighting the candelabra, c.1962

Above: Annie with friends in snow, c.1962. Below: Annie Wright with friends Ruth Ann Horvitz, Eric Gulley, Bart Gulley, and dog Turk, c.1962

Above: Rusell Wright, c.1962

SOUP (Over)

MENU #44

      IRISH LAMB STEW
      HOT ROLLS
      APRICOT WHIP OR
      CARAMEL CUSTARD

LAMB STEW   Order chuck of lamb, boneless. Ask butcher to cut it in 1" cubes.

Wash meat in cold water. Put in casserole. Cover with cold water and let it come to a boil. Drain water off. Rinse meat with cold water. Then put back in casserole and cover as before with water or meat stock.

Crush 1 clove of garlic. Put in spice bag with 1 bay leaf and 1/2 tsp of marjoram leaves. Add to stew.

Then add to stew: carrots & celery, diced, and small white onions and small peeled potatoes.

Let simmer until meat & vegetables are tender. Season with salt & pepper to taste.

To thicken stew, mix melted butter with sifted flour & stir in gradually.

Serve with cooked green peas on top of stew.

APRICOT WHIP

    3/4 cup stewed apricots   1 tbsp lemon juice
    1/2 cup sugar   5 stiffly beaten egg whites
    1/8 tsp salt.

Cut apricots very fine, add sugar & cook until sugar and cook until sugar dissolves, stirring constantly. Add salt & lemon juice and fold into egg whites. Pour into lightly greased baking dish and bake 30 minutes in 350° oven. Chill & serve with plain or whipped cream.

CARAMEL PUDDING
CUSTARD

    Follow directions on package of prepared pudding mix. Serve with plain or whipped cream.

SERVICE (N.Y.)

    Lamb stew in large brown stacking server
    Brown or gray dinner plates
    Gold & orange plaid cloth
    Rolls in basket with linen liner
    Dessert in brown bowls
    Clear glassware.

SERVICE

    Olive circular cloth   Stew in Shepherd's Purse Sauce Pan
    Shepherds Purse dinner plates, bowls for dessert.
    Rolls in covered basket.   Yellow glassware.
            OR
    Orange & yellow cloth.   Stew in White Clover Casserole
    White clover dinner plates, bowls for dessert.
    Rolls in covered basket.
    Yellow glassware.

MENU #51
AFTER THEATER SUPPER

    RICH MUSHROOM SOUP
    GARLIC BREAD TOASTED
    ASSORTED RELISHES
    BABA AU RHUM or COMPOTE
    COFFEE
    BRANDY

Recipes:

RICH MUSHROOM SOUP   (made in a blender)

    1 pound fresh mushrooms
    1/4 pound of butter (1 stick)
    4 cups chicken stock
    1-1/2 cups cream
    3 egg yolks
    salt and pepper

Wash and dry mushrooms. Cook in butter about five minutes. Cool.
Reserve 5 of the cooked mushrooms for garnish and turn the remainder into blender.
Add chicken stock, egg yolks and cream and blend until mushrooms are coarsely chopped
Turn the mixture into a heavy saucepan and heat slowly, stirring constantly until thickened
Season with salt and pepper
Slice remaining mushrooms in thin slices and float on top.
Serves 4 - 6

ASSORTED RELISHES   Raw cauliflower, radishes, jumbo ripe olives

BABA AU RHUM   Buy from delicatessen (canned) - If you can't find it at nearby delicatessen, Bloomingdale's always carries it.

    Add 1/2 to 1 cup of rum.
    Warm in double boiler

Service:

    Brought in on cart
    Red napkins
    Soup in Mary Wright tan colored soup tureen
    Mary Wright individual soups on Mary Wright matching plates
    Kitchen ladle
    Babas on Black Velvet platters served individually on Black Velvet salad plates
    Stainless soup spoons and teaspoons
    Coffee in Chemex over brass candle warmer
    Black Velvet coffee cups and saucers
    " " sugar and creamer
    Smallest glasses for brandy

MENU #41   RED CABBAGE SALAD
                                      HOT PRE-COOKED ROLLS
(Garrison Picnic)   RICE PUDDING or
                                          Raspberries and Cream Cheese or
                                          Raspberry Whip
                                      MILK, ICED TEA OR ICED COFFEE

SALAD   Combine the following with French dressing:
                Red Cabbage (slivered)
                Cooked tongue, or ham, cut in squares
                Swiss cheese, sliced.
                Seedless raisins
                Sliced hard boiled eggs
                Small amount of boned chicken

RICE   1/2 cup rice   1/2 cup sugar
PUDDING   3 cups milk   1/2 cup heavy cream
                4 lightly beaten egg   1/2 tsp. nutmeg
                     yolks   1 cup seedless raisins
                Grated rind of 1/2 lemon   (May be omitted)

                Wash rice well; combine in top of double boiler with
                milk. Cook, covered, over hot water 1-1/2 hours or
                until rice is thoroughly cooked. Comgine remaining
                ingredients. Blend with cooked rice.

                Bake in brown casserole in hot oven 400° until
                browned & set (about 15 minutes).

RASPBERRY   1 cup fresh raspberries crushed   1/4 tsp grated lemon peel
(or strawberry 6 whole raspberries   1½ envelopes unflavored
WHIP   3/4 cup ginger ale   gelatin
                2 tsp lemon juice   1/2 cup nonfat dry milk
                                                           powder
                                                  12 noncaloric sweetener
                                                           tablets

                Soften gelatin in 1 1/2 cup water; dissolve over hot
                water. Combine with ginger ale, crushed tablets, lemon peel
                and curshed berries. Chill til mixture begins to thicken.
                Combine lemon juice and ½ cup water in small bowl; sprinkle
                milk poser on top. Beat until stiff. Fold into
                gelatin mixture. Chill. Serve topped with whole berries.
                Serves 6.

SERVICE   Salad in large wood bowl, served on paper plates, or
                     wooden plates.
                Pudding in blue casserole in which it was cooked.
                     with small blue bowls.
                Beverage in paper cups, green glasses or white
                     plastic glasses.
                Rolls in basket.

                For guests: Cloth: Black & blue Moi or
                                     Blue striped plastic

MENU # 73   Four Blessings Meat Balls
                                      (They represent good fortune,
                                         prosperity, longevity & happy
                                         family life)
                                      Rice, Frozen Peaches, Tea
RECIPES:
                                      with sour cream or
MEAT BALLS   1½ lbs. coarsely ground pork   *fresh orange or tangerine*
                1 tsp. grated fresh ginger,   *in sauce of undiluted froze*
                1 tsp. salt.   COATING: *orange juice*
                3 tbsp. soy sauce   1/4 cup cornstarch
                2 tbsp. cornstarch.   1/4 cup water.
                1 tbsp. sugar
                8 water chestnuts, diced.
                1 tbsp. scallion, finely chopped
                1 cup crab meat, diced.
                2 egg whites, slightly beaten

                Mix pork, fat, ginger, salt, soy sauce, cornstarch,
                sugar, and water chestnuts together well.

                Add scallion, crab meat and slightly beaten egg
                whites to mixture.
                Heat 1/4 inch oil in a large skillet or chinese
                wok, shape the meat into four large balls or into
                individual balls using ½ cup per serving and.
                spread the cornstarch, water coating on the out-
                side of each ball.

                Saute meat balls, browning on each side and basting
                frequently with the oil. Remove meat balls and
                make the saude in the skillet.

SAUCE FOR
MEATBALLS   3 tbsp. soy sauce.   2 thin slices fresh ginger
2   2 cups chicken broth.
                1 tsp. sugar   2 tbsp. sherry.
                6 scallion tops   2 pounds fresh spinach.

                Combine all ingredients but the spinach in the
                skillet or wok; bring to a boil.

                Add meat balls and reduce heat, cover, simmer slowly
                for two hours (*)

                (*) For freezing, cook just 1 hour, pack in freezer cartons.

Wash spinach and pour boiling water over it. Drain well. Remove
meat balls to serving plate and keep hot. Add spinach to the Sauce
and cook until done. Remove spinach from pan, thicken sauce with
about 1 tbsp. cornstarch. Aarange spinach on a hot platter, place
meat balls on top of spinach then pour sauce over all.

Serves 8 to 10 people.

Recipe book, recipes and service instructions, Russel Wright, c.1955

Iroquois Shepherd's Purse, c.1961

Sprinkle top with shredded coconut.
Chill about 2 hours.

Take chilled pie out of refrigerator about
20 minutes before serving so crust will crispen
a bit.

Sprinkle a few toasted almonds on top.

SERVICE   Tan Indian Cloth & napkins   Brown
(N.Y.)   Cook & serve oysters in ~~yellow Casual China~~ casserole,
               ~~Yellow plastic plates.~~   Brown dinner plates.
               Salad in ~~large white glass salad bowl with~~ individual
               ~~small bowls.~~   wooden bowls.
               Dessert on ~~white glass plates~~   black plastic plates
               Rolls in long dark hinged basket
               Goblets for wine.

OYSTER CASSEROLE

1 LB. OYSTERS   1 tsp. Worchestershire
1 medium onion   1 tsp cayenne
1/4 cup sliced celery   1/4 tsp. pepper
1/4 cup capers   1/4 cup white, dry wine
1/2 can mushrooms   2/3 tsp garlic salt
3 ~~tsp~~ tbsp. flour   1/2 tsp salt
1/4 cup butter   1/2 tsp dry mustard

COFFEE JELLY

6 tsp. instant coffee   1 inch stick cinnamon
1 inch square orange peel   1-1/2 enveloped unflavored gelatin
1 inch square lemon peel   12 sweetener tablets
                                4 tsp. sugar
                                Add brandy

Soften gelatin in 1/2 cup water. Mix coffee, crushed tablets, peel &
cinnamon in 2-1/2 cups boiling water. Simmer 5 minutes. Add gelatin
and dissolve. Strain and chill. To serve, break up with fork.
Serves 6.

SERVICE   Olive cloth
(Garrison)   Oysters cooked in Shepherd's Purse Rry Pan
               Dark Brown Japanese dinner plates.
               Wood plates for salad.
               Orchid leaves plastic plates for pie.

MENU #19   BAKED OYSTERS
                                PRE-COOKED ROLLS
                                AVOCADO & GRAPEFRUIT SALAD
                                WHITE CHRISTMAS PIE
                                or CHOCOLATE ICE CREAM &
                                  WHITE CREME DE MENTHE WITH
                                  BLACK WALNUTS   CACAO

Recipes: WHITE WINE

BAKED OYSTERS: 1 quart oysters   1 tbsp. butter
                1/8 lb. bacon   1/4 lemon
                1-1/2 tsp. finely   bread crumbs
                  chopped scallions   salt
                1-1/2 tsp. finely   pepper
                  chopped parsley

Chop bacon as fine as possible and line a deep
  casserole with 1/3 of it.
Add layer of oysters, dust with salt and pepper,
  sprinkle with chopped scallions, chopped parsley,
  bread crumbs and more chopped bacon.
Add another layer of oysters and proceed as before.
Sprinkle with bread crumbs; dot generously with
  butter & bake in hot oven for 25 minutes.

SALAD   Slices of avocado & grapefruit sections on remaine
                  lettuce.

                Dressing: 1 part lemon juice
                           2 parts olive oil
                           salt & pepper

WHITE   1 envelope gelatin   1/2 cup whipped cream
CHRISTMAS   1/2 cup cold water   3 egg whites
PIE   1/2 cup sugar   1/4 tsp cream of tartar
                1/4 cup flour   1/2 cup sugar
                1/2 tsp. salt   1 cup moist shredded coconut
                1-1/4 cups milk
                1 tsp vanilla
                1/4 tsp extract

Soften gelatin in 1/2 cup cold water.
Mix flour, sugar, salt together in a saucepan, add
  milk, stirring well.
Cook over low heat, stirring constantly. Boil 1 minute.
Remove from heat & stir in softened gelatin.
Chill.
When partially set, beat with rotary beater until
  smooth.
Add vanilla & almond extract, then fold in whipped
  cream.
Beat egg whites, cream of tartar and sugar into a
  meringue; then fold into above mixture.
Fold in shredded coconut and pile into cooled baked
  pie shell.

(Recipe continued on other side)

Recipe book, recipes and service instructions, Russel Wright, c.1955

Margaret Spader and Russel Wright, *Life* magazine, 1962

Jack Lenor Larson (left) with Russel Wright, *Life* magazine, 1962

Russel Wright, upstairs mezzanine, c.1962

Living room in winter with Sonoma red cabinet, c.1962

Dragon Rock exterior, *Life* magazine, 1962

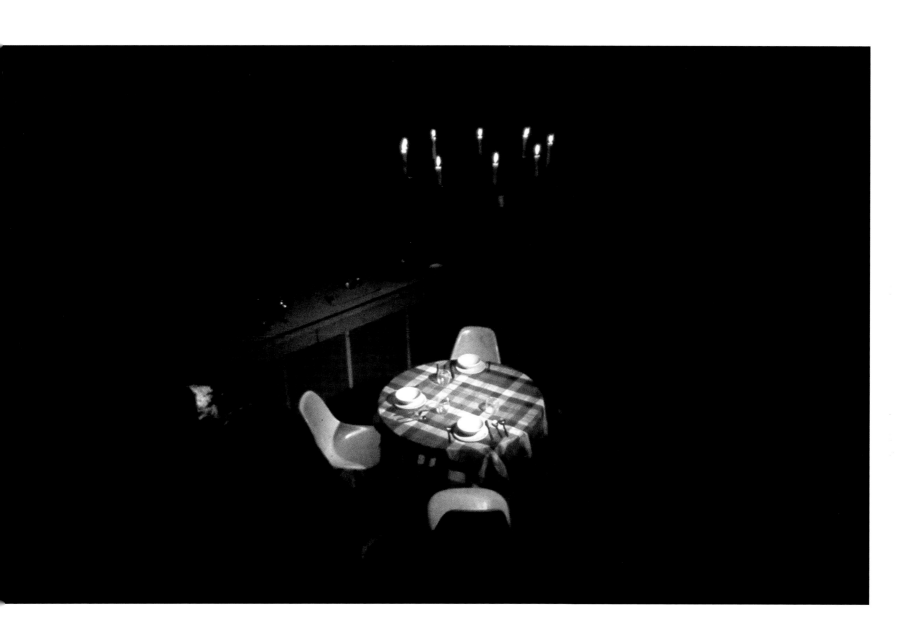

Dining room, nighttime with Simtex plaid tablecloth, c.1955

WOODLAND PATHS

MAJOR FEATURES OF THE TRANSITIONAL AREAS:

Autumn Path and Sunset Walk

Winter Path and Morning Walk

White Pine Path

Deer Pool Path

Trail to Lost Pond

Zigzag Trail, The Return from Lost Pond

Fern Meadow Path

Wickopee Trail

Kilalemy Trail

Laurel Field

Laurel Field, Upper Trail

Deer Run

Mary's Meadow

Wright felt strongly the closed, continuous quality of the forest landscape and realized that any kind of opening, no matter how small, created a noticeable change. Along his footpaths, he went out of his way to discover, enhance, or create a wide variety of gaps of different sizes, and to give each of these places a distinct identity, sense of spatial cohesion, and thematic unity. For this reason, each place has a name—The Deer Pool, Lost Pond, The Laurel Field—and this distinct identity is one of the aspects of Wright's designs that needs management to be maintained. These holes in the forest are used as the natural places of pause along the route, the special events of the garden where various pieces of the story of the life of the forest can be told.
— Carol Levy Franklin, *Manitoga Design and Management Guide*, 1982

When Mary and Russel Wright purchased the seventy-seven-acre forested grounds that comprise Manitoga, a slice of the side of a mountain, they set out to shape openings to the vistas, places to retreat

Mary Wright, Untitled landscape, oil on board, 1950

Fern meadow, photo c.1975

among the stately hemlocks, and a variety of ways to take in the massive quarry and the greatness of the Hudson Valley beyond. While Manitoga was designed initially as a summer retreat, it evolved to become a continuing dialogue with nature, seasonal forces, and unfolding evolution.

This exchange with nature became Russel's life's work until his passing in 1976. Manitoga—the local Wappinger tribe's name for Place of Great Spirit—is Russel's magnum opus, a landscape that he purposefully shaped, repaired, healed, and reclaimed. A local stream is rerouted to form a waterfall, and great blocks of granite are precisely oriented to define the cascades that fill a quarry pool. A rolling moss carpet frames a graceful stand of white birch. The canopy, formed by the massive trees on the higher slopes, leads down to mountain laurel, black huckleberry, and lowbush blueberry. Several regions of fern meadows are carved among the lower woodlands to create corridors of light, varying the forested mass. Mary's Meadow, a welcoming sunlit field at the base of the grounds framed in spring by blooming dogwoods, is the most manicured landscape feature, due to the removal of hundreds of trees. Some of the trails, which lead from the mountainous Hudson Highlands ridge across Manitoga and down to the river and were originally created by the Nochpeem Native American tribe, are still used today.

Manitoga is a synthesis of all of Russel's interests, an analysis of form and live theater, an undertaking at a massive scale, dynamically changing over time. The organic management of vegetation that Russel espoused is a pioneering blueprint for sustainable, environmental practices.

Mary's cousin Carol Levy Franklin worked devotedly beside Russel at Manitoga for many years. Upon his passing, she undertook an impressive manifesto about the grounds, which was underwritten by the National Endowment for the Arts. This document addresses the overall philosophy of the general design organization of the property and how each region unfolds in a choreographed sequence. Levy Franklin explores the many paths, their topography and their related ecological meanings. Her text is accompanied by a drawing or photograph of each section in its optimal condition, with a guide to best practices for long-term maintenance.

When the Wrights came upon the land of Manitoga the forest was dense. The quarry was a neglected overgrown cavern, filled with debris. Fulfilling Mary's primary wish for the site, Russel first cleared and damned the quarry, transforming it to a gracious swimming hole. It became a dramatic reflective centerpiece, with a boulder at its center to serve as a platform for diving and sunbathing. The seventy-seven acres and circuit of events that comprise Manitoga are operatic in scale. Russel learned by walking the grounds in a daily meditation, studying the evolution over the course of seasons and throughout the years. As he navigated the site's perimeter, winding through the various elevations and observing the contours, patterns, and outcroppings, a slowly emerging narrative unfolded. Cascading terraces were revealed, boulders cleared of growth disclosed their massive architectural presence, branches were pruned to shape the light and were varied for dramatic intrigue and pause. Spaces were created to form a raw yet considered sequence of rooms, not unlike those of a Japanese villa garden. The varied materials including bridges formed by broad wood planks, to granite stairs and stepping stones, evoking a sense of adventure.

Instead of imposing rigid forms and preconceived patterns on the place, Wright sought to make contact with the fluid structure and connecting patterns of the natural world. Wright saw Manitoga as a living organism and respected its processes. He waited for the place to reveal itself to him and delighted in the complex order that unfolded over time. Were he alive today, Wright would undoubtedly recognize that Manitoga embodies a systems view of the world which is based on the fundamental wholeness and interrelatedness of all phenomena.
—Carol Levy Franklin, 1987

Through instinct and insight, Russel pioneered a sustainable environmental practice of land management using only native species, shunning any invasive or nonorganic mediations. His innovations and stewardship continues to be studied today. Russel Wright listened, and collaborated with nature, embracing the power of its forces, allowing for spiritual connection and reconciliation. He willed the property to the public, hoping to teach us what he had come to understand. Wright's humble observation and respectful dialogue with nature revealed a moral and ethical wisdom to live by.

Joe Chapman, Manitoga Trail Map, 1969

Dogwoods in bloom, Mary's Meadow

Mary Wright, etching, c.1948

Mary Wright, etchings, c.1948

Margaret's Waterfall, c.1980

Baldev Raju and coworker, c.1970

Above: stone steps. Below: bridge, c.1970

Quarry pond stone steps, c.1980

Autumn Path, c.1980

Quarry stream, winter, c.1980

Grasses in snow, c.1980

Seed pods in snow, c.1980

Above: Dogwood in bloom. Below: Annie's terrace, c.1975

Above: House on quarry outcrop. Below: triple oak, c.1975

Russel Wright in his oak seat, c.1972

Sweet Woodruff, Annie's terrace, c.1980

Martha Graham Girls birch grove, c.1980

Ferns and lichen, c.1980

Russel Wright among the ferns, c.1975

Russel Wright, c.1972

ACKNOWLEDGMENTS

I first initiated this project upon meeting with Annie Wright in a noisy coffee shop in Manhattan on April 17, 2019. There we affirmed our affinity for one another and the richness of her parents' untapped story.

My first foray into researching this publication was conducted at Russel and Mary Wright's Syracuse based archive in November 2019. Folder upon folder, box after box, revealed decades of creativity and productivity, when their design practice and partnership sprang to life.

Late February of 2020 I returned to the East Coast for an intensive research trip. This included a pilgrimage to Dragon Rock, where I met its exceptionally gracious steward Allison Cross, director of Manitoga / The Russel Wright Design Center, who is developing innovative programming while shepherding Dragon Rock's maintenance and welfare.

I enjoyed a most special day with Joe Chapman at his very special home and a private, intimate tour of Dragon Rock. From there I drove up to the Center for Photography at Woodstock, where the Maverick Festival archive is maintained. This was followed by a glorious day with Annie Wright, greedily pouring through her extensive personal archive. I spoke and met with the intrepid collectors Bill Straus and Gary and Laura Mauer, great experts on the known and more arcane projects produced by Russel Wright Associates. Bill's specialty is lamps, and the Mauers produced a thoughtfully considered book on textiles.

I had intended to return to the East Coast to visit David Leavitt's archive, photograph the property throughout the seasons, and meet with landscape architect Carol Levy Franklin and Baldev Raju—Russel's gardener and loyal friend who accompanied him during the last weeks of his life. Little did I know that my first major exploratory excursion would be my last. That trip concluded March 8th, 2020, before life as we knew it changed with the arrival of COVID-19. To be honest, I am going to press with extensive research supplementing our collective understanding of the Wright's with added depth, albeit it is not exhaustive. I feel the topic here warrants further inquiry, but I am proud to share this foundational knowledge.

Russel and Mary Wright haven't received a retrospective since the Cooper Hewitt, Smithsonian Design Museum's exhibition in 2001, now two decades past. And it is surprising how relatively few people have visited Dragon Rock at Manitoga, given its proximity to New York City. If possible, I urge you to experience it for yourself.

One anecdote I wish to share concerns this book's white cover. Frankly, white wasn't my first instinct, particularly given the sumptuous color palette of American Modern dinnerware and the spectrum of options the collection provides. But white is the color of Russel's Formica desk. In lucid contrast to the natural wood and the range of materials present throughout his home, his desk has a stark white sheen, a tabula rasa, the clean slate, and clarity from which to imagine. Further, white is the color of Snow Glass, an elusive, coveted, special production of a combination of glass and porcelain, which retains nuanced qualities. It is the ultimate expression of Wright's genius, where mass production meets imperfection, embracing naturally occurring phenomena. Annie Wright recounts:

> *Manufacturers had spent decades trying to get the bubbles out of glassware, and here Russel Wright was trying to put the bubbles back in. A tough sell, at every turn. But, we all knew, that kind of design taboo never stopped Russel. And, my father's determination was always relentless. So, manufacturers would scratch their heads but forge ahead.*
>
> *And it all proved to be a difficult sell. At one point, an important client, I believe it was Neiman Marcus, was running out of its stock of the American Modern line at a rapid clip, so, they desired more product as quickly as possible. Irving Richards agreed to provide additional inventory of American Modern immediately if the store would agree to take a shipment of Snow Glass as well. They agreed only to dump the entire shipment of Snow Glass into the Rio Grande. This could have had an impact on Snow Glass's availability. I do know that it is a difficult find for collectors, and it was only used in our house for cherished guests.*

I am greatly humbled to have earned the trust of Annie Wright, who granted the right to tell this story of her parents. She has witnessed many projects and efforts come and go, and her confidence in me was essential. This is a story shrouded in ambiguity. Annie knew Mary for only two years before her mother passed, and I have sought to capture Mary's keen charisma and creative largesse. I have great empathy for Russel; I am impressed by not only his abundant talent but also his continued powers of renewal and assertion of principles. He survived the pressures of his parents' expectations, and effectively navigated an era when one needed to obscure aspects of their identity. He must have been overwhelmed by the loss of Mary, finding himself a widower with a young child to raise and a design empire to uphold. He was a loving parent and surely did his best. I would like to say to him, "you did good." It is no surprise that Annie has built a life for herself as a talented chef and a nurturing parent while managing a storeroom that can barely contain her parents' legacy. She serves dutifully on the board of Manitoga / The Russel Wright Design Center, her childhood home that bears her father's name. I would like to propose that adding Mary's name to the center is worthy of discussion.

I recognize that attribution is a delicate matter. One thing we know for certain is during the prevailing culture of the mid-twentieth century, women were restricted to be architects or designers. Within the famed partnership of industrial designers Charles and Ray Eames, contemporaries of the Wrights, Charles was the celebrated figure. Even in 1991, the Pritzker Architecture Prize was awarded to Robert Venturi without mention of his wife and collaborator Denise Scott Brown, which remains a contested wound.

I wish to thank Jennifer N. Thompson, my editor at Princeton Architectural Press. I am graced by her receptiveness, encouragement, generosity, and care in bringing this book to fruition. I was breathless, flush with findings, when we first met, and she has maintained her spirit for the project through every threshold.

I wish to express my sincere gratitude to everyone who supported this project and helped bring it to fruition. There are many intelligent hands who have informed the book's development, and each was essential. My hope was to synthesize a range of accounts to evoke a rich, open exploration while inviting additional scholarship. The publication aims to preserve culture, this special human legacy, by honoring the Wrights' story and their marks with respect and care.

THANK YOU

Annie Wright, heir, Board of Directors, Manitoga/The Russel
Wright Design Center

Joe Chapman, Russel Wright's significant other, from 1964–1976,
Director Emeritus, Manitoga/The Russel Wright Design Center

Allison Cross, Executive Director, Manitoga/The Russel Wright
Design Center.

Carol Levy Franklin, landscape designer, author, Manitoga
Management Guide

Jennifer N. Thompson, Executive Editor, Princeton Architectural
Press

Lynn Grady, Publisher, Princeton Architectural Press

Paul Wagner, Design Director, Princeton Architectural Press,

Janet Behning, Production Director, Princeton Architectural Press

ARCHIVES

The Burke Library at Union Theological Seminary, Columbia
University Libraries, Leah Edelman, Outreach Archivist,
Meredith A. Self, Preservation Reformatting, p. 34

The Center for Photography at Woodstock, New York, Gaede
Striebel Archive, Hannah Frieser, Executive Director, Sarrah
Danziger, Digital Lab Coordinator, pp. 10, 13, 18, 19, 20, 21,
22/23, 24, 25, 26, 27, 28/29, 30, 3`, 32, 33, 36/37

Garrison Art Center, Katie Schmidt-Feder, Executive Director, pp.
186, 187

Manitoga/The Russel Wright Design Center, Vivian Linares,
Director of Collections, Interpretation & Preservation, Sarah
Connors, Outreach/Visitor Services Manager, Emily Phillips,
Landscape Collection & Preservation Manager. All images
courtesy of Manitoga/The Russel Wright Design Center,
Garrison, N.Y., pp. Cover, 6, 46, 54, 58, 59, 60, 64 top, 68, 69,
73, 79, 91, 92, 93, 94, 96/97, 98, 100, 101, 102/103, 104,
106/107, 108, 111, 112/113, 114, 115, 116, 117, 119, 120, 121, 122,
124 right, 125 left, 128 left, 130, 131, 132, 133, 136, 140, 144,
145, 148, 150, 153, 154, 155, 157, 158/159, 160, 161, 162, 165,
166, 167, 170, 172, 173, 174, 175, 176, 177, 180/181, 184, 185,
188, 189, 190, 191, 192, 193, 194, 195, 196, 197, 198, 199, 200,
201, 203

Smithsonian Archives of American Art, Alexander Archipenko
papers, 1904-1986, bulk 1930-1964, p. 15

Russel Wright Papers, Special Collections Research Center,
Syracuse University Libraries, Nicole C. Westerdahl, Reference
and Access Services Librarian, pp. 40, 44, 45, 52, 61, 67, 71, 72,
74, 75, 76/77, 78, 80/81, 82, 83, 85, 86, 87, 88/89

Wright Auctions of Art and Design, Richard Wright, pp. 42, (lower)
48/49, 50, 51, 56/57

DESIGN AND EDITORIAL

Simon Johnston, Design Consultant

Ximena Amaya, Design Execution

Hyu Oh, Assistant Designer

Clare Jacobson, Editor

Meg Whiteford, Editor

PHOTOGRAPHERS

Adam Anik, pp. 55, 64 below, 101 right, 199

Emily Beets, Ripley Auctions, p. 66

Frank Famularo, pp. 186, 187

Alexandre George, Interiors, 1961 pp. 144/145, 154

Jennifer Golub, pp. 118, 123, 124 left, 125 right, 126, 128 right,
129, 135

Farrell Grehan, Life Magazine, 1962, pp. 150, 153, 155, 157,
158/159, 160, 161, 165, 166, 167, 172, 173, 174, 176

Robert Glenn Ketchum, p. 122

Sophie Kovel, pp. 127, 134

Vivian Linares, pp. 64 above, p. 79, 128 left, 185

George Patanovic Jr., p. 163

Newman Schwartz, p. 8, pp. 100 left, p.188, 197 top

William Tefft, p. 189

Ronald Thomas, p. 170

COLLECTORS

Kim Kovel and Al Eiber

Mary Sahm Knauff

Laura and Gary Mauer

Bill Straus

GRATITUDE

Freya Clibansky

Madeleine Cuotrona, New York Foundation of the Arts

Lisa Diebboll, Highland Studio

Chris and Patrick Grehan, Farrell Grehan Estate

Lee and Whitney Kaplan, Advisors

Sophie Kovel, Researcher, The Maverick Festival

Laura Kurgan, Advisor

Anne Skomorowsky, Researcher Helen Flanders Dunbar
andAllison Stokes

Tal Vigderson, Intellectual Property Consultant

Edwina von Gal, Sustainable Landscape Advisor

Joe Weston, Contracts Manager, Princeton Architectural Press

Dedicated to Mel Golub